ADVANCED SKATEBOARDING

A Complete Guide
to Skatepark Riding
and Other Tips for
the Better Skateboarder

Messner Books by LaVada Weir

SKATEBOARDS AND SKATEBOARDING
The Complete Beginner's Guide

ADVANCED SKATEBOARDING
A Complete Guide to Skatepark Riding
and Other Tips for the Better Skateboarder

THE ROLLER SKATING BOOK

ADVANCED SKATEBOARDING

A Complete Guide to Skatepark Riding
and Other Tips for the Better Skateboarder

by LaVada Weir

Photographs by Al Moote

Julian Messner

New York

Library of Congress Cataloging in Publication Data

Weir, LaVada.
    Advanced skateboarding: a complete guide to skatepark
riding and other tips for the better skateboarder

    SUMMARY: Discusses areas of interest to the accom-
plished skateboarder including competitions, skateboarding associations, skateparks, and difficult
maneuvers.
    1. Skateboarding—Juvenile literature.
[1. Skateboarding] I. Moote, Al. II. Title.
GV859.8.W43 1980   769.2'1   79-16801
ISBN 0-671-33011-X lib. bdg.

Also available in Wanderer Paperback Edition

CONTENTS

ACKNOWLEDGMENTS   7

FOREWORD   9

1. Born of Necessity   11

2. What to Expect at a Skatepark   17

3. Skatepark Rides and Runs   26

4. Rate Your Park   39

5. Techniques of Park Skateboarding   45

6. Tricks on the Terrain and in the Air   57

7. Riding Equipment   76

8. Safety Gear   89

9. Mind and Body   96

10. Competitions   111

11. Skateboard Associations   117

12. Skateboarding Around the World   123

GLOSSARY   125

ACKNOWLEDGMENTS

My appreciation and thanks to the many who contributed their expertise to make this book possible and to these persons in particular: Kathie Bomeisler, Deanna Calkins, Yvonne Cucci, Pam Duimstra, Rob Feiger, Chris Foley, David Heady, Russ Howell, Mike Johnson, Bob Judd, William Koester, Sally Anne Miller, Betty Mitchell, Seb Molina, Stacy Peralta, Steve Rikard, Ken Rogers, Sandy Saemann, Kelly Selby, Jim Shilling, Jay Simpson, Paul Sims, Amy Stevens, Louis Velasquez, Florence Vincent, Ron Wall, Cindy Whitehead.

My special thanks to the skateboard parks which opened their doors to me and my photographer: Big O, 157 North Wayfield, Orange, CA 92666; Runway, 19401 South Main Street, Carson, CA 90745; Skateboard World, 4445 Emerald Street, Torrance, CA 90510; Super Bowl, 2605 Airport Drive, Torrance, CA 90505.

My gratitude to the following associations for the information they supplied: Canadian Pro-Am Skateboard Association, Number 1-149 West Nineteenth Street, North Vancouver, B.C. V7M 1X3; International Skateboard Association, 711 E7, West Seventeenth Street, Costa Mesa, CA 92627; New England Skateboard Association, Box 851, Greenfield, MA 01301.

I wish also to acknowledge the assistance found in these magazines: *Skate & Surf*, 474 Laurel Canyon Boulevard, Suite 208, North Hollywood, CA 91607; *Skateboard Industry News*, 15720 Ventura Boulevard, Encino, CA 91346; *Skateboarder Magazine*, Post Office Box 1028, Dana Point, CA 92629; *Skateboard Magazine*, 14 Rathbone Place, London W.1, England.

A special mention to these shops for their cooperation: Kanoa Surf, 702 Deep Valley Drive, Rancho Palos Verdes, CA 90274; Pro-Am Skate Shop, 20 Peninsula Center, Rolling Hills Estates, CA 90274; Pro-Am Skate Shop, 936 North Western Avenue, San Pedro, CA 90732.

A deserving thank-you to the manufacturers for their contributions to my research: American Cycle System, 1449 Industrial Park Street, Covina, CA 91722; Flex-Tred, Wooster Products, Inc., Spruce Street, Wooster, OH 44691; Forlor, Inc., BSC Trucks, Post Office Box 1024, Saratoga, CA 95070; Gordon & Smith Skateboards, 5111 Sante Fe, Suite E, San Diego, CA 92109; Great American Skateboard Co., 2630 South Shannon, Santa Ana, CA 92704; Gull Wing, 1080 West Bradley, Suite F, El Cajon, CA 92020; Hobie, Post Office Box 812, Dana Point, CA 92629; Lip Slider Inc., Post Office Box 6075, Orange, CA 92667; Logan Earth Ski, 742 Genevieve, Suite

Q, Solana Beach, CA 92075; Mr. Seb Sportswear Inc., 1161 East Twelfth Street, Los Angeles, CA 90021; Pan Western, 17985 Sky Park Circle, Suite B, Irvine, CA 92714; Quazar International, Inc., 17450-F Mount Herrmann Street, Fountain Valley, CA 92708; Ramp King Inc., 10335 Jovita Avenue, Chatsworth, CA 91311; Rector Skatewear, Post Office Box 371, Graton, CA 95444; Sims, 835 East Canon Perdido, Santa Barbara, CA 93103; Skatepads, 837 Robert Kiester Place, Goleta, CA 93077; Sky Hooks Hawaii, Inc., Post Office Box 30369, Honolulu, HI 96814; Sports Inc., Post Office Box 483, Newport, RI 02840; Van's, 704 East Broadway, Anaheim, CA 92805; World Skateboard Team Corporation, 935 Activity Road, Suite ''J,'' San Diego, CA 92126.

And most of all, my indebtedness to Lee M. Hoffman, my editor, who had the patience and fortitude to see me through another skateboard book.

FOREWORD

As managing editor of a publication read by thousands of skateboard retailers and manufacturers worldwide, I am delighted that someone finally got around to writing a how-to book for experienced skateboarders.

Skateboard technique has come a long way since the 1960s, when being able to ride a board without falling off was itself a major accomplishment. Today, thanks to an assortment of advances in both technology and design, the skateboarder can perform maneuvers which, only a decade ago, would have been considered impossible.

In fact, the skills of many skateboarders have become so considerable that by the time 1984 rolls around, skateboarding may be ready to try its wings as a full-fledged event in the Los Angeles Olympics. And who knows—readers of this book may be among the first participants in such a history-making event.

For that to happen, of course, there will have to be nationwide competitions leading, as with other sports, to Olympic qualification. This will require the formation of local skateboard leagues at the grass-roots level, complete with uniform rules, judging standards, eligibility requirements, etc.—all under the direction of an overall governing body for the sport.

But this is still in the future. For the present, I commend to the reader's attention Ms. Weir's fine book and . . . SAFE SKATEBOARDING!

Mike Miller
Managing Editor
Skate & Surf

"Flying"!

1
Born of Necessity

The music is playing. The skatepark is open.

Skateboarders in their bright-colored safety gear are working out in the park. "Ripping it up," they call it. They look as if they are flying.

"Look, Ma. No gravity!"

One skateboarder, wearing a red helmet, is working the *pool*. He shoots up the side to the rim above the blue tile. Three wheels of his *board* are whirling in thin air. He hangs there like a held breath. And then, turning his board on one wheel, he drops back smoothly into the pool, only to repeat the ride up the other side.

Three wheels are whirling in the air.

Another skateboarder rides what appears to be a paved, deep channel which winds its way through the park. First, she gives a strong push to get going fast. Then she shoots up the *bank* to cut a straight line along its side. She is *carving* the banks. Farther down the channel is a section which looks like a concrete pipe with the top half taken off. She cuts into the pipe and rocks from side to side, turning her body each time while still in the air above the side of the pipe. Rocking, turning in the air, rocking again—her rhythm is as steady as a pendulum swinging in a clock. She's *boinking*. There's a *bowl* at the end of the pipe. She shoots out of the pipe and into the bowl to carve its sides. Her body hangs almost straight out from the side of the bowl.

Today's skatepark riders seem never to have heard of the law of gravity.

No Place to Go

Skateboarders back in 1970 were the first to feel that they were close to flying on their own power. *Polyurethane* wheels had just

Yvonne Cucci at Super Bowl, working out the pool. *Boinking*, some call it.

come on the market. The new wheels had a gripping power that almost let the skateboarder ride right up the wall.

But where were the walls?

Skateboarders discovered the sides of dry storm drains, reservoirs, swimming pools, and all sorts of forbidden places. Just as quickly, the police discovered them, too. It was against the law. And there was the chance skateboarders might be hurt or even killed. But where were they to go?

Wipe Out?

Most skateboarding accidents happened on surfaces never intended for skateboarding. The accident rate climbed. Injuries reported now were more severe. Nevertheless, enough skateboarders continued to ride the forbidden places. They gave a bad name to all skateboarders. Some communities banned skateboarding entirely. It looked like a repetition of the old *clay-wheel* days of the mid–1960s. All skateboarders were in grave danger of being wiped out, one way or another.

$$$$

But they were not the only ones. Manufacturers of skateboarding equipment had the same fear. They knew they would lose a great deal of money.

It was a strange situation. The manufacturers were guilty of improving a product. And because the skateboard was improved, it allowed the skateboarder to do more on it. The problem was that there was no place for the skateboarder to ride safely or legally.

In 1974, a group of Ventura, California, high school skateboarders pointed the way. They petitioned their city council for a legal place to skateboard. The result was a free municipal skateboard park, perhaps the first *skatepark* ever. It was nothing fancy or exciting.

Somewhere along the line, someone—no one knows for sure who—solved the problems of the skateboarder and of the manufacturers. The solution would prove to be an opportunity for many others, too. Whoever it was listened to skateboarders describe their ideal place for skateboarding. They designed the skateboarder's dream: bowls, pipes, channels, and other runs and rides. Someone added money and built the design in smooth

One of the very first skateboard parks. Carlsbad, California.

concrete. They put a fence around it, charged admission, and so a skatepark was born.

A Wave of Concrete

By 1976, concrete began curling in like the perfect wave of summer. Commercial skateboard parks appeared almost simultaneously in California, Florida, Texas, Australia, and Japan. In two years time, thousands of skateboarders were riding in the parks.

At last, skateboarders no longer needed to be in the streets. They were out of the storm drains. Skateparks were the answer.

2
What to Expect at a Skatepark

It's a great day for skateboarding. You pack your equipment and off you go.

Park Admission

Your membership application is in your pocket. It is all filled out. Because you are not yet 18, the form is signed by your parents. You have read the rules of the park printed on the application. The first time you went, you didn't know that besides paying admission, you had to become a member to get into the park. For those who are from out of town and plan to ride only once or twice, the park charges more than if you are a member. In the long run, it pays to be a member.

It's a great day for skateboarding.

At the entrance counter, you present your membership application and your money for a one-year membership. The admissions clerk takes a Polaroid picture of you and writes your name and your emergency phone number on the back. It is put on a card

NAME ____ LAST _____ FIRST _____ MIDDLE

ADDRESS _____ STATE _____ ZIP ____

CITY _____ BIRTHDAY ____ MO/DAY/YEAR

PHONE NO. _____ HAIR ____ EYES ____

HEIGHT _____ WT. ____

SIGNATURE OF PARENT OR GUARDIAN IF UNDER 18

A standard application for Skatepark Membership.
Courtesy Super Bowl, Torrance, California

Super Bowl 1 So. Bay

2605 Airport Drive Torrance, Ca. 90505

RELEASE OF LIABILITY

1. In consideration and upon payment of a non-refundable membership fee for the grant of a license by SUPERBOWLS OF AMERICA ("Licensor") for the use of its facilities for skateboard operation and for viewing others operating such equipment, the undersigned liability arising out of Licensee's use of or presence upon the property of Licensor. This Release extends to Licensor, together with all subsidiaries, affiliates, successors-in-interest, and, Licensee agrees never to sue any or all of such persons or entities in heirs, assigns and legal representatives) of Licensor, officers, directors, employees and agents (and each of their respective connection with any cause of action of whatever kind for injuries to the person of, or damage to the property of the executive management only such injuries and/or damages as may result from the gross negligence or willful misconduct of the executive management of Licensor.

2. Licensee, his heirs and legal representative, agree to indemnify Licensor against any damages, causes of action, claims, judg-ments, costs of litigation and attorneys' fees, which may result from Licensee's use of, or presence upon the property or facilities of Licensor, including injuries to the partners, officers, directors, employees, or damage to the property of Licensee's use of

3. Licensee agrees that he will comply with all rules and regulations as may be posted within the Park relating to Licensee's use of Licensor's property and facilities.

4. Licensee agrees to promptly leave the property of Licensor whenever requested to do so by an employee of Licensor, for what-ever reason.

5. Licensee agrees that he or she is not an agent or authorized representative of Licensor and that the license only confers the priviledge to use the facilities in accordance with the rules and regulations of Licensor.

6. Licensee understands that skateboard riding is a dangerous activity and is fully aware of the risks and hazards inherent in entering upon said premises or in participating in any events held in or upon said premises and hereby elects voluntarily to enter upon said premises, knowing the present condition and knowing that said condition may become more hazardous and dangerous during the time that he or she is upon said premises. Licensee hereby voluntarily assumes all risks of loss, damage, or injury that may be sustained by him or her, and any damage to any property of the licensee while in or upon said premises.

7. Licensee hereby authorizes Licensor and its representatives to photograph, televise, videotape or otherwise record the image of Licensee while he or she is using any facility, or is upon the property of Licensor, and to use such visual records or Licensee for any purpose, including commercial advertisements.

AUTHORIZATION FOR PATIENT'S RECORD(S). I, the undersigned, do hereby authorize any hospital, physician, or other person who has attended me or examined me to furnish to SUPERBOWLS OF AMERICA or its representatives, any and all information with respect to any illness or injury, medical history, consultation, prescriptions or treatment, and copy of all hospital or medical records.

A photostatic copy of this authorization shall be considered as effective and valid as the original.

AUTHORIZATION TO TREAT A MINOR. I (We), the undersigned parent, parents, or legal guardian of the below named minor, do hereby authorize and consent to any X-Ray examination, laboratory procedures, anesthetic, medical or surgical diagnosis and treatment, and emergency hospital care which is deemed advisable by and is to be rendered under the general or special supervision of a member of a medical staff, or emergency room staff under the provisions of the Medicine Practice Act, and on a staff of a general hospital holding a current license to operate as a hospital or clinic from the State of California, Department of Public Health. It is understood that this authorization is given in advance of any specific diagnosis, treatment or hospital care being required, but is given to provide authority and power to render care which the aforementioned physician, in the exercise of his best judgment, may deem advisable. It is understood that an effort shall be made to contact the undersigned prior to rendering treatment to the patient, but that any of the above treatment will not be withheld if the undersigned cannot be reached. It is also understood that the person presenting this authorization is acting as my (our) agent and will not be held liable for treatments rendered.

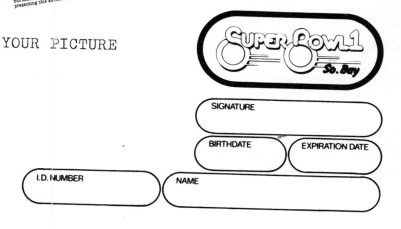

YOUR PICTURE

Super Bowl 1 So. Bay

SIGNATURE

BIRTHDATE   EXPIRATION DATE

I.D. NUMBER   NAME

A membership card waiting to be filled in. *Courtesy Super Bowl, Torrance, California*

and laminated in plastic so that it won't get crumpled from carrying around. The card is kept in the park files while you are riding. The clerk gives you a ticket to pin on your clothes to show that you have paid.

Membership Benefits

Now that you are a member, you are given a decal to put on your board. Your first riding session is free. After that, you will pay admission for each session of riding. A session at most parks is 2 hours. If you want to ride for only an hour, you pay half the admission fee. Every month you will receive a park newsletter. It tells what special events—contests and demonstrations by professionals—are coming up and skateboarding news in general. This park has a large *pro shop* where you can buy new equipment, parts and safety gear. A member gets 10% off all purchases from the pro shop.

Not every park gives all of these benefits with membership. Some parks give other benefits. Each park is different. This one has a snack stand selling hot dogs, fruit juices, soft drinks, and ice cream. Also there is a game arcade featuring pinball, foosball, and video machines.

Equipment Inspection

The admissions clerk directs you to the Safety Patrol Monitor for Equipment Inspection and Skill Rating. The monitor will check your equipment each time you come to the park.

You pass the bins containing the safety gear. Anyone who skateboards in a park must wear safety gear—helmet, knee and elbow pads, wrist guards, and gloves. You have been riding for some time now and have your own. Nevertheless, you look in the

The safety monitor checks your equipment.

bins to see if there is old, worn, or cheap safety gear. You've heard that some parks rent them out. Although the gear for rent here is not as nice as yours, it's good enough to protect the skater.

The safety monitor is easy to find. He's wearing a bright red cap and shirt with *Safety Monitor* sewn on the pocket and across the back in white. He looks at your equipment. You are proud of your gear because you keep it in top condition.

He sees that the *rims* of your board are smooth, not splintered. The *deck* is completely covered with *grip tape*. The *trucks* are tightly bolted to the board, not loose. The *bushings* have hardly been used. The wheels have the proper spin. You adjusted them last night, but you carry your skate wrench to make adjustments, just in case. Naturally, your wheels have *sealed*, or *precision*, bearings. Some skateboarders still have old-fashioned wheels

You have passed inspection and get a sticker on the top of your helmet to prove it.

with *loose* bearings that can spill out on the pavement and send everyone crashing. Parks will not allow them.

The monitor smiles and nods when he hands your board back. "Nice board," he says. "Let's see how good you are."

Skill Rating

Because this is your first time at the park, you must take a skill test. It's almost like taking a test to get a driver's license. Your park membership card will be punched to show whether your skill rating is novice, intermediate, or advanced.

This park has separate riding areas for each rating. Three colors are used to tell one from the other. You get a button to wear which is the color of your rating. You must stay in your own area. As you get better, you can get your rating changed.

The skill rating test is given in the *freestyle* area, which is large, flat, and slightly banked around the edges. You are wearing your wrist guards, ankle guards, elbow, and knee pads. Now you put on your helmet, fasten the strap, and pull on your gloves.

"What do you want me to do?" you ask.

"Just ride," the monitor says.

You set your board down and move off toward the small bank. You give a little push, climb the bank, do an easy *kick turn* at the top, roll back down, do a tail wheelie on the flat terrain, and finish with a 180.

"More?" you ask. When the monitor shakes his head, you flip the board and tuck it neatly under your arm as you've seen Russ Howell (the internationally famous "King of Skateboarding") do.

The monitor gives you an advanced rating button and grins at you. "I knew from the way you set your board down and moved off you were advanced," he says. "Don't try to rip it all apart on

Cameron Ainley passes the skill test easily and is rated for the advanced area.

the first day,'' he cautions. He's all right. You're going to like it here.

The monitor punches the time on your ticket to begin your 2-hour session. You glance at the clock. You have done a lot since you came in, but it has taken only 10 minutes. It's worth it. You know that everyone else skating in the park has equipment that passed inspection and rides in the area right for them. It's time to look over the rides and runs.

3
Skatepark Rides and Runs

The perfect skateboard park has not yet been built. So you need to look at a park the first time and ask yourself, "Can I have fun here? Or will I get hurt?"

The fun and the safety of a skatepark depend upon two things: its design and the way it is run.

Ron Wall, manager of a $1.5-million park in California who has a strong background in the use of safety equipment, puts it this way, "Skateboarding is a safe sport. It is potentially a dangerous sport." He draws a comparison between it and a gun.

"You learn an awful lot about a gun before you pick one up and shoot it." So you have to learn all about skateboarding, parks, and competitions if you are going to be active in it.

THREE AREAS

Ideally, a park should have 3 areas. One area is the novice, or beginner; another is the intermediate, and a third is the advanced.

If you are a beginning skateboarder, it is easy to see why you would want a safe place to learn and not get in the way of others. Once you are riding comfortably, you will want a place where you can improve your skills and learn new techniques.

If parks are not new to you and you are skating well, you will want runs and bowls that you can enjoy riding. And you will want other rides that offer you a chance to work up to something new.

Novice Area

This is an area mostly for beginners, and usually doubles, to provide flat space for freestyling. The flat area alone should measure at least 40 by 80 feet. The sides should be banked to stop the rolling boards of either novice or freestyler. The novice also uses the banks for practice.

Another ride is the bowls. These are small with gradually sloping sides. The banks and runs should not be too large for small skateboarders. The runs are mild and *mellow*.

One park features a horseshoe-shaped run which is like a sidewalk with curved sides. If you are a beginner, you can learn by sitting on the board and riding it all the way. After you get the

Novice area. Mike Johnson, manager of the Big O, warms up in the freestyle area. Mike is no beginner. After losing a leg in a Motocross accident, he turned to skateboarding. He has won championships in every competitive event.

A horseshoe-shaped run which is like a sidewalk with curved sides.

feel of riding, you can try it standing on your skateboard. Then try going up the curved sides. With practice again and again, you can go on to the next step.

Intermediate Area

This area may have some or all of the following rides: snake runs; moguls; vortex bowl; pool; pool bowl; small, or open, 1/2 pipe; and a *slalom* course.

Snake run, as its name suggests, is a run with continuous curves. Both sides are banked.

Mogul run has snake curves with a mogul added. The mogul is a large bump of concrete on one of the convex curves. When you go over it, it gives you added thrust and you are pushed ahead.

Vortex bowl is a challenging bowl about 10 feet deep. But in it you can learn bowl riding at any depth. By riding in the bottom,

How's this for a snake run? With moguls, too. The Big O.

it is like riding in a shallow bowl. As your technique improves, you can try riding higher up the sides. It has no vertical terrain.

Pool bowl (similar to a pool, described below under Advanced Area) is a combination between a pool and a bowl. It is a square-shaped pool that has no vertical terrain. However, the skating surface is almost vertical to give the skater the opportunity to work up to handling true verticals. The risk of burning or crashing is higher here.

The open 1/2 pipe can be in an intermediate area if it is *very* open. Imagine a pipe split lengthwise with the top half removed and the remainder laid back slightly. That is the open 1/2 pipe.

The slalom run is a stretch of smooth pavement down a hill. The sides are banked slightly. The end is also banked. Some slalom runs are wide enough for two riders to race down head-to-head. The slope is about 6 percent grade, and the runs are

Mike brushes up techniques on the slalom run.

from 200 feet to 500 feet long and 20 or 30 feet wide. Many runs have spectator areas for the slalom.

Advanced Area

The most challenging rides are to be found in here. Expert technique is required. The opportunity for *radical* riding is in this area. *Radical* means riding the verticals. In the advanced area there may be a cloverleaf, pools, keyhole pool, capsulated pool, deep bowls, 1/2 pipe, 3/4 pipe, and full pipe.

A *cloverleaf* is an arrangement of 3 or 4 shallow bowls joined by a mogul in the center. Looking down at it from a helicopter, it

The cloverleaf is an arrangement of 3 or 4 bowls.

resembles a large cement cloverleaf. If the bowls are no deeper than 6 feet, an intermediate skater can work them with practice. The mogul in the center thrusts you from bowl to bowl. You can ride almost effortlessly and endlessly.

Pools are round and deep, built like a backyard swimming pool, with *coping* and tile. The coping is the rounded *lip*, which sticks out about an inch from the top of the pool. A true pool also has tile—that border of hard, slick tiles along the top rim of the pool.

A *keyhole pool* is a pool with a special entry way, which resembles the bottom of a keyhole. The top of the entry is about 3

A keyhole pool has a special entry way.

feet wide, and then it rapidly narrows down to a space just wide enough to allow you to drop into the bowl. It is a quick entry.

The *capsulated pool* looks like a cold capsule split open lengthwise.

Deep bowls may be as deep as 15 to 19 feet. There are many different shapes—round, oblong, kidney, fruit bowl.

Pipes are just that—concrete pipes. The pipes in the advanced area differ from the open pipe of the intermediate in that they have vertical terrain. A 1/2 pipe will have from 1 to 2 feet of vertical. A 3/4 pipe may have as much as 4 feet of vertical. There should never be more than 4 feet of vertical anywhere. More than that is too much of a risk.

Looking at one of the closed ends of a capsulated pool.

Mike shows off the 3/4 pipe.

Where does the *vertical terrain* begin in a pipe? As you know, vertical means straight up and down. Imagine the face of a clock. To give you a picture of the cross section view of a 1/2 pipe with verticals, add lines straight up from the 9 o'clock and 3 o'clock positions. For a 3/4 pipe, the verticals would begin at the 10 and 2 o'clock positions. In both cases, the bottom of the pipe is rounded.

35

A *full pipe* can be ridden like a 1/2 or a 3/4 pipe, except that it does not have verticals. The ultimate challenge of the full is in riding the top. Only a few *extremely expert* riders attempt to do that. The risk factor is very high.

Kele Rosecrans, age 7, Van's team member, tries out the full pipe. *Photo courtesy of Van's Skateboard Shoes*

A *tombstone* is a vertical piece of concrete about 2 to 4 feet high and about 4 feet wide. This slab is placed at the top of a bowl or bank at the end of a slalom run.

A tombstone is a vertical slab about 2 to 4 feet high.

Variations and combinations of all these features appear with almost every new park. Among park builders, news travels fast, and they take ideas from each other. Because each new park tends to be an improvement over the ones built before, the skateboarder is offered more fun at less risk.

Unfortunately, there are exceptions. Not all the second generation parks (parks built since the original ones) are improvements. Some of them do not meet the design requirements of expert skateboarders. Other parks are not run properly. There are older parks which are safer simply because they are managed better. But how are you to know?

4
Rate Your Park

Parks should build many safety features. Some you cannot see. Others you can see at a glance on your first visit to the park.

Emergency Entrance

The park should have a driveway or parking space marked Emergency Only.

Let's be realistic. There will be accidents. They happen in every sport. Some accidents require care from the paramedics or a trip to the hospital. If you were hurt, you'd want to be sure the proper medics could get to you in a hurry.

The best arrangement is a park designed so that an emergency vehicle can be driven directly into any area. The Big O Skatepark in Orange, California, is designed like this.

Every skatepark should also have a first-aid station. It should be easy to get to from both the park and the street.

Safeguards

The spectator area should have a good view of the runs. It should be located far enough from the riders so that they will not be distracted by spectators. The area should have a fence which protects the spectators from flying boards or falling riders.

Soft safety netting (not chain-link) enclosing each run prevents boards from flying from one run to another when a rider falls. An excellent example is the use of elasticized netting strung between posts which are on garage door springs. The springs are anchored upright in the ground with plastic tubes slipped over them. The tubes are cut near the base so as to allow the spring to bend with the weight of a flying board or falling rider.

There should be walkways around the runs so that the riders can get from one run to another without getting in the way of others using the run or the walkway.

If the park is open for nighttime skating, the lighting should be placed to light up the area evenly. It should not shine in the skateboarder's eyes.

A good park, as described in chapter 2, will have separate areas for novice, intermediate, and advanced. The areas will be color-coded. Some park managers feel that, because skateboarders police themselves, area restriction is unnecessary. Nevertheless, the color coding is an extra safeguard.

Another safeguard is posted reminders such as those used by The Runway in Carson, California: Wait Your Turn! No Dropping In, No Crossing Lines, No Trains. Their skate patrol enforces these rules.

Good safety netting can catch a flying board or a falling rider without injury.

One simple safeguard, which you can see at a glance, is cleanliness. Litter on the runs causes accidents. No food, drinks, or smoking should be allowed in the riding area of the park and signs should be posted to that effect.

Unseen Problems

A park can look safe and still have problems the skateboarder cannot see but should know about beforehand. Skateboarders are good about passing the word along to other riders. Professional skateboarders do the same, only on a larger scale. When they get invitations from all over the United States and abroad to give demonstrations and to enter competitions, they rate the parks and bring back descriptions such as whether they were fun to ride or too dangerous to enjoy.

When professionals give a demonstration—a pro demo—in your town, go not only to observe, but also to ask the experts how your park rates and about other parks you may plan to visit.

Skateboarders describe park runs as ''gnarley,'' bowls as ''kinky''; transitions are ''sharp,'' or ''mellow.'' A ''mellow'' park is the highest rating they can give. What do they mean?

A *mellow* park means that it is *not* a dangerous park. It is a

A *mellow* park.

park you can enjoy. The *transitions* are those areas between the vertical and the bottom of a run or a bowl. *Mellow transitions* are gradual and continuous curving without abrupt or *sharp* changes. *Gnarley* means the pavement has spots of concrete which are harder than the concrete around them. *Kinky* means a hard ridge, or line, within the concrete. Both are caused by concrete which was not poured continuously and not worked out until completely smooth.

Gnarls and kinks are not visible, but you can feel them when you ride over them. Deanna Calkins, an International Skateboard Association (ISA) Pro Rider, describes the experience. ''When you come up a wall and hit a kink, your legs bounce. It holds you back or throws you off.'' She offers this advice. ''If the park or ride is new to you, ask others how the cement is. They will tell you if there are gnarls or kinks and where they are so that you can avoid them.''

Around the Curve

One of the most serious problems to overcome in designing a skatepark is the traffic control. Sometimes, to get more runs into a park, they are laid out in such a manner that more than one run feeds into a common area. The result is collisions.

Before entering a run, take time to study its traffic control. Take turns with the other riders. Avoid collisions.

On park design, Sally Anne Miller, executive director of ISA, advises that there should never be more than 4 feet of vertical; pools should be perfectly symmetrical; coping should not stick out too far; and the freestyle area should be at least 40 by 80 feet. Skatepark builders hire ISA Pro Riders as consultants in planning parks.

Park Management

"However," says Director Miller, "a park can be beautiful, even designed for safety, but if it is not managed and supervised properly, there will be a lot of accidents. On the other hand," she points out, "a park can be quite radical—dangerous looking—but because it has excellent supervision, the accident rate there is lower than at the mellow park."

The well-managed park hires expert skateboarders who have Red Cross First Aid Certification for its safety monitors. Safety monitors are on duty at all times. A first-aid kit is kept at each of the runs.

The equipment inspection and skill rating test, as described earlier, is standard policy at a well-managed park.

These management practices protect the skateboarder and make better business for the skatepark. If your closest park does not have them, you might suggest them in a friendly, interested way. You might even get yourself a good job if you meet the qualifications to be a safety monitor.

5
Techniques of
Park Skateboarding

It's time to skateboard.

There are three general kinds of skatepark riding: pool, which involves banks and bowl riding, slalom, and freestyle.

Banks + Bowls = Pools

Most skateboarding will be riding variations of banks and bowls. Banks vary from the small, shallow ones around the freestyle area, where the beginner learns about banks, to the steep ones which you find in the snake runs and the moguls for the intermediate and advanced skateboarders, and, finally, to the pipes and pools for the experts.

Naturally, the steeper the banks, the more experienced you must be to ride them. Riding the very steep banks and riding high up in the deep bowls and in the pools—in other words, riding the verticals—is *radical* riding. Skateboarders call it simply *rad* riding.

Rad riding ability depends first upon mastering the techniques of riding banks and bowls. The expert adds the artistry of *aerials* to achieve continuous fluid motion. (Aerials are described in chapter 6.)

How to Ride Banks

To approach the bank, use a push-off start with the toe of the front foot placed just back of the wheels and pointed straight ahead. When you get up enough speed, place your other foot across the tail. Now, pivot the front foot so that it is parallel to the back one.

Compress your body (stoop to bring your body closer to the board) slightly before you go up on the bank. Use your arms to balance. As you come up to the top of the bank gradually, nose your way back down, leaning your body in the direction you wish to go. When you come up a bank, expect a feeling of weightlessness.

Before progressing to steeper banks, there are certain skills which you must first understand: weight and unweight; the kick turn; and frontside and backside.

To *weight*, you compress your body, bending your knees to bring your body closer to the board. To *unweight*, you come up, straightening your knees. The amount of bending and unbending you do depends on how much weighting and unweighting you feel you need. To further unweight, as at the top of a steep bank

Yvonne Cucci *weights* her body as she hits the tiles and is turning to reenter the bowl.

She is *unweighting* as she comes up the side of the pool.

or bowl, throw your arms up. "The theory," says tall, lanky fifteen-year-old Jay Simpson, a skate patroller at Skateboard World in Torrance, California, "is that the more of your weight you can throw in the direction you want, the less you have dragging behind you that you don't want."

The *kick turn* on a bank is the same as the kick turn you do on level terrain. With both feet across the ends of the board, weight the tail to move the nose around to the direction you want to go. Set the nose down and go.

Frontside or *backside* is determined by whether you are facing the wall you are riding (frontside), or riding with your back to the wall (backside).

In the novice area, a young skateboarder approaches the bank to do a *kick turn* at the top.

To ride steep banks, use the same foot position as for other banks. Go into the back frontside, unweighting as you start up the bank, do a kick turn at the top, and come down backside. Lean into the bank as you're going in. Don't lean forward on your board. Going up frontside, you must decide where to make your turn, because after the turn you cannot see where your back wheels are. Turn before you lose momentum. To achieve style, try to make your kick turn on the last possible fraction of terrain left at the top edge without your wheels hanging up on that edge.

Kathie Bomeisler goes into the bank *frontside* ready to make her kick turn.

Here she goes into the bank *backside*.

Be careful not to set your board down too quickly after the kick turn. Set it down when you feel you are starting your roll down.

Riding Bowls

Moving from banks to bowls, bowls allow the less-experienced skater to stay low on its walls and not hit too steep an angle. The most advanced skaters can get up their speed to the point where they can skate almost vertically to, or straight out from, the wall. You have to have speed to ''stick'' to the wall. The ones who fall are those who try to get too high on the wall before they have enough speed to stick there. In other words, you must create centrifugal force. Webster's Dictionary defines *centrifugal force* as being ''that force which tends to impel a thing, or parts of a thing, outward from a center of rotation.'' The greater the speed, the stronger the centrifugal force. Your speed is throwing you outward and the wall stops you from going farther. To borrow a phrase from science fiction, you could say, ''You are stuck by the Force.''

Kathie gets ready to make the transition from the bank to the level in the channel.

Now on the level and ready to come up the other side.

Riding Channels

The greatest difference between riding a channel and riding on level terrain is that a channel always slopes on the sides. The skill in riding channels successfully is making the transitions from the bank side to the level bottom between banks and then up the other bank.

In teaching the techniques of bowl, bank, and channel riding, Kathie Bomeisler, ISA Pro Rider, says, "It is all in knowing when to bend your knees. Bend down on the way down; straighten up when you come up." She explains, "You bend the knees to absorb shock in transitions, to adjust balance, and to press a turn." *Press a turn* is holding your knees together and turning them in the direction of your turn. On channel riding, she cautions, "When entering a channel, don't start up too high or you'll put yourself in the position of having to make a sudden drop into a narrow spot at speeds you might not be able to handle."

Snake Runs and the Mogul

When you feel you have mastered both frontside and backside turns and can make transitions, you are ready to try the snake

The higher you go in the snake run, the faster you travel.

runs and the mogul. Both have sharp turns that allow you to build up speed. The higher you go on the sides of the runs, the faster you will travel.

The mogul has the addition of the big bump, a raised mound in the run or on a bank at the curve. After you have become acquainted with the run, you may want to use the bump to give you more speed.

To get the most speed from the mogul, *crouch* when you go up on the side of it. The lower you crouch, the more thrust you get when you come down. This action is the important pumping technique which you will use in the 1/2 pipe and in the full pipe.

Carving

The snake runs and moguls are great for carving the walls. *Carving* is to ride all four wheels on the cement, all the way through, weaving from one bank to the other without making kick turns. It's all curves. You can carve either frontside or backside.

Runs end in a bowl into which you can carve. When you carve into a bowl, keep your circle going. Then when you feel you are losing momentum, it's time to make a kick turn. Head down toward the bottom, weight and unweight to come up high. Make another kick turn and repeat the ride down and up as long as you want to ride it. When carving bowls, you should set your feet between the trucks. Then reset them with a foot on the tail for making your kick turns and riding the banks.

Skateboarders take turns at the runs and bowls. The rule is one rider in at a time. Those waiting for a turn watch to see when it is safe for the next rider and call out the "All Clear." Your turn is over when you lose your board or your momentum. The one exception to more than one in at a time is in contests when there are doubles. Then there are two at a time in the bowl.

The 1/2 Pipe

From the mogul, you can go on to the 1/2 Pipe, where you will approach a little of the vertical and the hard edges. The *hard edges* are the tops of the pipe.

It is easier to carve in a 1/2 Pipe if you get up a lot of speed coming in from the channel. It is difficult to carve in a pool without doing a kick turn to start up your momentum again. You can start up cold in a 1/2 Pipe by pumping, but that is doing it the hard way.

In the 1/2 Pipe, you can count on a constant curvature. It is more consistent than a mogul. The mogul may have a 30° curve on one side and a 45° curve on the other. When working the 1/2 Pipe, you are approaching vertical.

In working the pipes, it is very important that you have strong pumping skill. To develop it, begin by coming into the pipe fairly low. It's not so far to the bottom if you lose your board. As you get stronger and better, you can try for greater heights.

Wentzel Ruml is an ISA Pro Rider and champion rad rider who has conquered the banks, pipes, and bowls. He says, ''The important thing about riding banks, pipes, and bowls is to know when to bail out.'' His motto, which is echoed by every champion in the sport, is Go for What You Know.

6
Tricks on the Terrain and in the Air

There are many tricks and techniques which you can add to your skatepark riding. Some of them are done with four wheels on the terrain, others with one or more wheels in the air. When both the skater and the board are off the ground, it is an aerial. Skateboarders call it *airborne* or "getting air." The highest scoring maneuvers in competition are aerials. All these tricks and techniques are performed in competitions. They can be combined into a routine for freestyling.

The Drop-In

A *drop-in* is one kind of entry. Whereas the entry into a snake run begins more or less gradually down a slope, a drop-in is done by entering straight in over the edge of a pool, bowl, or 1/2 pipe. Often it is a vertical drop. Naturally, you go very fast. Immediately bend your knees, compressing yourself to absorb shock and to be ready to go up the other side. Unweight as needed when going up to assist your momentum. Kick turn at the top for your return or be prepared to start carving.

The Roll-Out

The *roll-out* takes place when you come over the top of the lip. You roll out on the lip for a second and then roll back in. Some parks have a nice, wide lip for smooth roll-outs.

This maneuver is done instead of a kick turn. It can be done frontside or backside. If you roll out frontside, out of a pipe or a bowl, it means you are facing the wall. It is easier if you roll out backside, because then your back is to the wall and when you drop in, you are facing the drain and are in a position to see where you are going.

Variations can be added to the roll-out, such as aerials.

Roll-Back

The *roll-back* is a deceiving maneuver. You come up on the wall and, instead of doing a kick turn and coming back down, you lift your front wheels and start rolling backwards on your back wheels. Then you whip your front wheels back around, set them down, and continue down.

Fakie

When working the 1/2 pipe, do the roll-back instead of a kick turn at the top. Pick up your momentum by pumping and continue to rock in the 1/2 pipe. Continued rocking is called *rockabyes*.

360° Fakie

You can do a 360° after a fakie. A 360° is a complete spin with the nose wheels in the air. Weight the tail, throw your arms in the direction of your circle, and spin. About the only 360° you can do on a vertical is off a fakie.

A 1 1/2

A 1 1/2 is done the same way as the 360° with a 180° added to it so that you are headed down the bank again. You can do any number of 360°s, 720°s, and add a 180°.

Many of the standard freestyle tricks, if done on the banks or on the vertical, rack up points in competition and thrill the spectators.

Pirouette

The classic pirouette is to jump up from the board, spin around, and come back down. The board stays facing in the same direction during the spin. It can be done on level terrain or on a bank.

One of the many variations is the Closed Spin Pirouette. It is

done by making your spin while you have been riding on one leg.
Spin and land on one leg.

Powerslide

The powerslide is done at high speed. Turn the board so that

Kathie practices a powerslide.

the wheels slide sideways and continue riding in the new direction.

360° Slide or Reversal

Wentzel Ruml, sharing credit with co-riders Jay Adams, Tony Alva, Bob Biniak, Paul Cullen, Shogo Kubo, Jim Muir, Peggy Oki, and D. Oldham, has perfected—''wired down''—the 360° slide or reversal on a bank. Imagine making a complete body circle on the side of a bank. Ruml says that it took a long time, with everyone working on it, to perfect. This is the way it's done.

First of all, the terrain must be a 40- to 70-degree slope with a round bottom. (1) Approach the bank with plenty of speed, then set your feet directly over both sets of wheels (2) Hit the bank with lots of momentum behind you. Squat. (3) Place both hands on the cement and shift your weight to pull your body around. (4) Keeping your wheels on the cement, put your weight on your hands and your front foot. You are now pulling your body around and facing downhill. Because you are at the halfway point, you feel a slight, drifting sensation as your feet and board roll in above you. (5) Your speed has reached its peak. Your wheels break loose. Relax and let your body follow the flow of the board. (6) Place your hands higher up on the bank and get ready to thrust yourself downhill. (7) Use your hands and arms to straighten up and to balance yourself on your board. Make sure your feet are directly over the wheels and your body weight is evenly distributed over the board in order to make a smooth, controlled downward ride.

AERIALS

Kick Flip

The *kick flip* is a slight aerial. It is making the board do a complete horizontal flipover while the skater is in the air. Begin with one foot on the board, pushing up the rim of the board with the other. As you bring your foot up, hook the rim of the board with the side of your shoe (use that bulge on the side of the foot where the big toe joins the foot), and lift the board. As you lift, jump into the air. The board does a complete flipover and you land back on the deck. You can combine this with other techniques to invent new tricks.

Bunny Hop

The *bunny hop* is another small aerial. It is a jump made while coming out of a bowl or a 1/2 pipe. When you reach the rim coming up out of a bowl, push off with your feet on the board and at the same time grab the nose of your board with one hand and pull, lifting the board up in front of you. Once you coordinate your movements, it will appear as one fluid movement. It's a neat way to come out of the bowl.

Tail Taps

Tail taps—or tail tappers—are pivoting on the tail of your board, not on your wheels, when you have come all the way off the wall. Grab the nose, pivot on the tail, and drop back in. Your wheels will be all the way out of the bowl.

You can pivot without using your hands by compressing your body and pushing off the wall. It is a matter of individual style.

To work up to tail taps, first practice grabbing the nose of your board when you are on the level in the freestyle area. Then work up to grabbing the nose and turning when only part way up the bank of the freestyle area. Continue to work up to steeper grades.

Steve Cathey of G & S pro team demonstrates a tail tap at La Mesa Skatepark. *Photo by Jim Goodrich/Courtesy of ACS*

One-Wheeler

You're doing a *one-wheeler* when 3 wheels are in the air above the lip, and you are turning on your back wheel. Work up to it from doing 180°s on the level to doing them on the wall, to finally making a last, split-second turn on the rim with all your weight on one wheel.

Anthony Sena clearly shows a one-wheeler on Van's ramp. *Photo courtesy Van's Skateboard Shoes*

Nose 360°

A *nose* 360° is a 360° turn on the nose of your board, with all 4 wheels in the air.

Airborne Reentry

Airborne reentry is coming back into the bowl or pool after you have done an aerial.

Dorian Rosecrans, age 9, makes an airborne reentry. *Photo courtesy Van's Skateboard Shoes*

Tandem Kick Turn

This trick involves 2 riders, each on a board, who sit facing each other with feet braced against the rims of the other's boards. Hands are locked. Start down a slalom slope which has the end of the run banked. The aerial comes into play as you approach the wall. Your pulling back starts your partner up the bank. His pulling back swings you around and up the wall. Gravity takes over, and you roll back down to the bottom of the bank. Sometimes you are able to get one more swing around on the way down.

Pipe Flyout

In a *pipe flyout*, you fly out from the side of the pipe into a bowl or channel.

Kathie is getting the hang of doing floaters before trying them out on the pipe.

Lipper 360°

A *lipper* 360° is doing a 360° on the lip of a bowl.

Floater

A *floater* takes place when you're coming down the sides of a pipe on the 2 back wheels. The front ones are floating. Since coming down on 2 wheels is not as stable as coming down on 4, you get the sensation of suddenly falling.

Boinking

Boinking is the technique of riding the 1/2 pipe up one side and down, and then the same on the other side. Petite, sixteen-year-old Yvonne Cucci, who rides for Van's, is an amateur champion and an expert boinker. She comes up the bank and while, as she tells it, "I am getting air (all 4 wheels in the air), I grab the rim at the middle of my board, and shift my body to reenter backside." Yvonne says she began by practicing picking up her board while riding in the driveway at home. "It takes a lot of practice—every day," she stresses, "if you want to be good."

High Jumping

High jumping is one of the events copied from track and performed on a skateboard. A high bar is used, as in track. The trick requires a long board—most are made of metal and have a lot of flex (flexibility, or springiness) so that you can get a strong bounce. Start bouncing before you get up to the bar. Think of it as springing on a diving board. The object is that on the last bounce, you get the thrust you need from the board to help you bounce up. Your board goes under the bar. At the same time, you jump. crouching your knees up to your chest to get as much height as possible. You land on the other side of the bar on your board.

Barrel Jumping

Barrel jumping requires 2 boards—a flex board and a strong wood board. Lay barrels down side by side. Plastic trash barrels are about one and one-half feet in diameter. Use the strong flex

Kathie does a high jump over a bench, letting the board roll under to the other side where she will land on it. *Courtesy of Kathie Bomeisler*

board to make your jump from, but land on the strong wood board. Once in the air, stretch your legs forward toward the landing board to clear the barrels.

Board in the Air, Too

High jumps, barrel jumps, and other aerials can be done with an attachment added to the skateboard. There are 2 styles. One is a pair of knobs bolted to each end of the board just back of the trucks. These are called *Air Schooms* and are for performing jumps, aerials, and handstands. The other style is *Sky Hooks* which can be used to do the same tricks. They are 2 curved, wide, polyurethane hooks which are attached to the nose and tail. For aerials, the pressure of your feet against them holds the board with you. When you want to be free of the board, just release the pressure.

Sky Hooks attached to each end of the board. *Courtesy of Sky Hooks of Hawaii*

Milton Taira "gets air" using a pair of Sky Hooks. *Courtesy of Sky Hooks of Hawaii*

Slalom

Slalom races are as much a favorite in skateboarding as they are in skiing. You race downhill while weaving in and out between cones set along the course. There are two slalom patterns: the straight line and the switchback, for which the cones are staggered. The spaces between the cones are called gates. In a contest, the racers are penalized for each cone they knock over by adding so many seconds to their time. The one with the shortest time from start to finish line is the winner.

Slaloming is a good technique to practice to develop your skateboarding skill. It involves right and left turns and weighting and unweighting. The body movement is basic to skateboarding.

SPECIFICALLY FOR POOLS

Axle Grind

An axle grind is a one-wheeler, with the axle grinding (scraping) along the lip before you bring it back in. If you want to do axle grinds, put on wide axles. They are best performed on the coping.

Edger

An edger is a variation of a one-wheeler, but instead of putting the full wheel on the bank, you ride on the outside edge of your wheel on the very top. Some riders prefer a hard wheel rather than a soft one, but it is strictly personal preference. The skater's ability is what makes the difference.

Chris Foley, slalom champion. Note the body alignment with the slalom run. *Photo by Cindy/Courtesy of Chris Foley*

Lip Slide

A lip slide is a slide maneuver along the lip of the bowl or pool. You go toward the lip. As you near the top, you snap your body around so that your rear wheels hit the lip. The thing to avoid is getting your trucks hung up. You are lip sliding only if your back wheels go over the lip. The board makes a 180-degree and then rolls back in.

Sometimes the banks around the freestyle area slope down to the level and have a nice lip for practicing.

Riding the Tile

Riding the tile is riding that 6- to 8-inch band of highly glazed, smooth tile which borders the inside of a swimming pool. The trick is again centrifugal force—enough speed to make you stick there. Tile riders prefer the small tiles which set up a rapid clickety-clack, clickety-clack, as all 4 wheels ride over them. The larger tiles make only a clack-clack clunk, which is not nearly so exciting.

Riding the Coping

The most difficult trick of all is riding the coping. Every pool that has tile must have coping. You can ride the coping on 2 wheels, or with 2 wheels on the coping and 2 on the tiles.

Stacy Peralta, Ty Page, and Steve Alba are champion riders of the tile and coping. They have worked their way up gradually to rad riding. In answer to the question, "What advice would you give to skateboarders?'' Stacy Peralta said, ''If you want to keep skating, you gotta stay safe. Don't do foolish things like skateboarding in streets or without your safety gear. You might as well do it the right way, instead of being a tough guy.''

Howard Hood shows how to ride the coping. *Photo by Bruce Hazelton/Courtesy of Kanoa Surf*

7
Riding Equipment

The skateboard equipment market offers hundreds of items. Fortunately, most of the products are good, due to the use of constantly improved materials. In most cases, the engineering is good, too, because the designers are skateboarders, or former skateboarders. Then the idea is turned over to trained engineers.

One example is the Sims Company, a leading manufacturer of blanks and wheels. Young Tom Sims was a skateboarder who turned inventor. He is now president of this company and his father is the vice president.

Besides creating new designs, the company is concerned with improvement and quality. They sponsor *pro-am* teams which do research for them every time they ride. The Sims engineers get feedback from team members and act upon it.

The Sims example explains why the industry is so lively and offers such a variety of good products. Products that are not quality soon disappear as skateboarders pass the word on their giant grapevine.

So you can rely on products from companies whose names are well known. A few of these companies and their addresses are listed in the acknowledgements in the front of the book. But don't hesitate to ask around and make your own reliability poll. Sometimes a brand-new product will outperform all others.

Here, in general, are some guidelines on what components you need and why.

Selection

Skateboarding is a form of personal expression—an art. That means that most of your skateboarding time will be spent experimenting and perfecting. It begins with the equipment you buy.

First, determine what kind of riding you plan to do. Then select the blank (board), wheels, trucks, riser pads, skid plates, and whatever other accessories best meet your needs.

Blanks

Blanks come in laminated layers of wood, fiberglass, combinations of wood and fiberglass, and aluminum. The differences depend on the desired weight and length of board and amount of flexibility. Lighter boards are easier to handle in freestyling. Heavier ones are best for downhill racing. Most bowl and bank

A variety of good wood blanks.

riders choose a wood blank for the best combination of flexibility and stability.

Freestylers prefer a kicktail and so do a good many bowl riders. A *skidplate* can be attached for bowl riding if the board does not already have one built in. A skidplate adds to the life of your board. Some wood boards also come with built-in urethane *nose bumpers* to protect the nose.

Sizes vary from 27-inch to 6-foot lengths, most of the long boards being 20 to 33 inches. The extremely long board is a novelty item for downhill road skiing. The 27-inch is a favorite for freestyling. For slaloming, a 28-inch board cuts through the gates easiest. The 30-inch is favored most for park riding. Riders who are taller than 5 feet 6 inches may prefer a slightly longer length.

Park riding has brought about a preference for wider boards.

Boards that were usually 7 to 8 inches wide are now 9 to 10 inches. The extra width allows more room on which to move your feet, which you do in park riding.

The special for the "big feet" crowd is the 8-wheeler. It is a difficult board to maneuver, except by the very experienced. Its width of 13 or more inches gives the big-footed rider lots of room for footwork.

Some blanks come with the holes for the *base plates* pre-drilled. The distance between the trucks determines the wheel base. The distance from the nose to the holes depends upon the length of the board. The longer the board, the farther in from the nose tip the holes are. The distance from the nose for the average-length board varies between 3-1/4 and 3-1/2 inches. The distance in from the tail varies from 4-1/2 to 4-3/4 inches. The farther in the wheels are from the ends of the board, the more leverage you have and the less foot-maneuvering room. The closer the wheels are to the ends, the stiffer the response is to kick turns.

The wide 8-wheeler is gaining popularity for skatepark riding.
Courtesy Sims

The way Lonnie Hiromoto rides the coping with an 8-wheeler helps explain why. *Photo by Bruce Hazelton/Courtesy of Kanoa Surf*

Trucks

Trucks improved greatly once manufacturers stopped using scrap metal and began using fine tempered steel and aluminum alloys instead. At about the same time, the mid-1970s, they applied engineering principles to their designs to make trucks highly sophisticated.

Your first consideration in selection is the turn angle of the *axles*. Turn the board upside down and press down on one of the axles. If the tip of the axle goes down at a steep angle, the truck is designed to give you a quick turning reaction. The less the angle, the more drawn out your turns will be. Axle widths go from about 3 to 8 inches, except for unusually long boards which require even wider axles. The narrower ones make tighter turns. The combination you make with turn angle and axle width decides the performance. Use 3-inch axles for quick turns as in slaloming. Use wide axles in bowl riding for more surface on the wall.

The best design improvement was the introduction of shock absorbers—or bushings. Keep a close check on the rubber and

From the top: bushings, riser pads, and a variety of trucks with varying axle widths.

urethane bushings. They wear out and become cracked and frayed. Before they do, replace them for your safety and riding comfort.

An aluminum spacer is now available to allow even further truck adjustment. The better trucks are built to let you change the adjustment and the bushings from bowl to street to slalom riding. Aluminum spacers give a firmer ride.

Experiment with your truck adjustment. Once you feel confident with a trick—that is, you have it wired down—tighten your trucks. There will be less board movement, which gives your body more opportunity to move. And that's the whole point of it, isn't it; letting the board be an extension of your body?

When you have the trick wired down, loosen the trucks again and go radical. You will discover how much your body has learned. You'll feel more confident and much freer. If the park is new to you, start in with your trucks tighter than usual. You want no unnecessary movement to control until you know the terrain.

Attachments

Riser pads between trucks and blank give you more wheel clearance, which is especially important in slaloming. They also give a higher center of gravity and, therefore, a feeling of riding high. The pads come in various thicknesses.

Space blocks, wedgies, or rad pads can be added to change the geometry, or angle, of the truck.

The *truck protector* is a strip of metal or extra hard urethane which is bolted to the underside of the rear truck and the blank. Lip Slider, Truck Guard, and other brands protect the rear truck when doing lip slides. They prevent hangups on the lip.

Aerial attachments are for making high jumps, barrel jumps, and other aerials if you don't like leaving your board. These

How the stainless steel lip slider is attached. The manufacturer states that it strengthens the truck and reduces truck vibration. *Courtesy of Lip Slider*

The lip slider is designed to allow the truck unit to slide up and over curbs and coping. *Courtesy of Lip Slider*

attachments let you hold onto the board with your feet. There are 2 styles: Air Schooms and Sky Hooks. (For descriptions see page 70.) However, skateboarders have a difference of opinion about these attachments. Some like them; others say they are very dangerous. If you try them, proceed with caution.

Before moving on to the last component, a word about *grip tape*. It is absolutely essential that you have some sort of gripable surface on the deck of your board. A product called Worm Tape can be used to replace ordinary grip tape. It gives more gripping surface because it is coarser. Check it out before you next resurface your board.

Wheels

The first development added to the urethane wheel was to go from one size for all riders to wheels of various diameters and widths. Wheels vary according to what you want to ride and riding conditions.

Wheel diameters now run from 60 to 70 millimeters, with most riders preferring 65 millimeters. Wheel widths vary from 1-1/2 to 2-1/2 inches. The smaller diameter and narrower wheels are preferred by freestylers. Small wheels let you pivot more sharply. Park riders want large, double-radius wheels. They roll faster and are better for pool riding.

The next change in the wheels was in the degree of hardness of the urethane, called the *durometer*. Durometer measures from 75, the softest, up into the 90s. The softer the durometer, the more gripping quality the wheel has. Hard wheels roll faster on smooth, hard surfaces, but slicker riding surfaces call for more grip. Here you have to know your ability. Work up to the combination of speed and grip you desire. Soft wheels are better for rough surfaces and sharp transitions. Softer wheels have more springiness. Your choice depends upon what kind of riding you do and what you want the wheels under you to do. If you don't have a variety of boards and wheels and yet do all kinds of riding (serious riders have from 3 to 5 boards to meet their needs), an 80- to 90-durometer wheel would probably best suit your needs. New compounds are being developed to get a wheel that is harder yet still maintains grip, which is what everyone wants.

A further development came in the design of the edges of the wheel. No longer is your only choice a 90-degree, or "sharp" edge. Either the inside or the outside edge, or both, may be bevelled, or *chamferred*. These wheels are called *double radius*. The chamferred edge is preferred by some riders for making power slides. Also, if the edge has been bevelled, there is less chipping out and, therefore, less danger of getting hung up on the lip of a bowl. The sharp edge is still preferred by some for making sharp turns on the lip. The choice is up to you.

The *core* wheel with a magnesium center, which entered the market toward the end of 1978, claimed to give a more stable ride. It will undoubtedly not be the last development in a still-young industry.

Your choice of edges. Note (at lower center) a cross section of a core wheel.

Oddities

Other unusual adaptations appear on the market from time to time. A 6-wheeled skateboard was introduced which looks like a board with a very long kicktail. Where the board curves up, there is a third set of wheels. This board could change the routines of freestylers.

Each year someone comes out with a motorized version of a skateboard, missing the entire point of the sport.

To be taken more seriously is the snow skateboard. You can convert any skateboard into a snowskate by attaching two Snow

Joseph Walker tries out snowskates at Mammoth Lakes, California. Note how Snow Skate is attached to a regular skateboard.

Skates over the wheels of your board. These skates are like wide skis made of tough polystyrene. The manufacturer claims you can downhill race, slalom, and do some freestyling with them. Then there are also the ice blades, called Hot Blades, to use in place of wheels.

The Wind Skate offers an attachable sail. The attachment is aluminum and the sail is nylon. If you live where there is a stiff breeze and wide, smooth places, such as a parking lot, playground, bike paths (if these are legal for skateboarders and not occupied), desert dry lake beds, or frozen ice lakes, your answer may be blowing in the wind.

A skateboard regatta in the parking lot. *Courtesy of Wind Skate, Santa Monica, California*

8
Safety Gear

Since 1977, protective clothing expecially for skateboarders has been manufactured. Buddy Allred, captain of the San Bernadino County (California) Safety Demo Team for Pepsi, advises, "All skateboarders should wear full gear—helmet, knee and elbow pads, wrist guards, gloves and athletic shoes—the works, even if only messin' around in your driveway."

Safety Gear. Top row: three styles of helmet. Note the protective padding inside the center one. Second row, from left to right: Hobie wrist guard, two styles of plastic (fiberglass) cup knee and elbow pads. Bottom row: a pair of leather and padded palm gloves (at left), and fabric knee and elbow pads (at right).

Helmets

Skateboarders complain that the helmets, constructed of polyurethane and padded with foam rubber, are hot and heavy. Although foam rubber does hold heat, it is still the best padding. Helmets being made now have the padding at only the impact points—around the head and over the ears. The rest of the area is ventilated.

One example of a very good helmet is the Kanoa Fly-Away helmet. It is made of hand-molded fiberglass with a special padding which keeps it light, but protective. It has good ventilation. Even though light, it is one of the strongest helmets made. The manufacturer calls it ''impact free.'' This means that there is nothing about its design or construction to catch. If you land on your head, the helmet deflects the force of your fall.

Bicycle headgear does not give adequate protection for bowl

The Kanoa Fly-Away helmet, an example of good protection. *Photo by Bruce Hazelton/Courtesy of Kanoa Surf*

riding. It is all right for freestyling. When you're looking around for head protection, spend a few dollars more and get the right kind of helmet.

Knee and Elbow Pads

There are two types of knee and elbow pads. One is completely soft. It is like a heavy stocking with extra padding at the impact points. Some have a rough leather covering on those areas.

The all-fabric pads are comfortable. The disadvantage is that often in the case of a fall, the concrete grabs the fabric and pulls it off while you are still skidding along.

The other style has hard plastic cups to cover the elbows and knees. In a fall, it will absorb a lot of the shock as well as stay on as you slide.

Gloves

These come in either all leather or leather on the palm side. There is padding in the palm area to absorb shock. Gloves protect you from abrasions only.

Wrist Guards

Next to the helmet, wrist guards are proving to be the most important item of safety gear. Over 35 percent of accidents in skateparks are to the wrists.

Ron Wall, Big O Skatepark Manager, says: "The most serious wrist injuries occur not so much in a break. A break usually occurs to the hand or arm, rather than to the wrist. The most serious injuries are the sprains, where the ligaments are torn and the tendons are torn off the actual bone. It is a whiplash, or twisting action."

Everyone is bound to take a fall sometime. "How," you ask, "can you prevent serious injuries?"

"Beginners," Ron answers, "tend to put their hands out in front of them when they fall. Learn to fall to the side and back and roll with your fall. Tuck your hands and forearms in close to your body, and take the fall on the fleshy parts of the body, like the upper arms, the thighs, and the buttocks. Wear wrist guards in case you forget."

The wrist guard wraps around the wrist. There is a thumb slot. It is padded. The padding on some models is thin, and on other models, such as the Hobie, the padding is thick sheep's wool. Inside the padding are two strips of curved aluminum—steel, in some models. One strip is bent to fit the contour of the palm, and the other is bowed to fit the back of the hand. On impact, the curved metal deflects the pressure.

In purchasing a pair of wrist guards, consider cost, comfort, and engineering design. The Hobie is well-designed and gives top protection, but it is the most expensive. The Sanjon, at approximately half the cost, is also well-designed and protective. It doesn't have the Hobie's heavy padding and is, therefore, less bulky.

Other models are merely wrist guards which orthopedists use at hospitals, but with the name *skateboard* on them, the price is doubled. Notice how the guard wraps around your wrist. Good ones give your wrists added support.

If you have to choose between gloves and wrist guards, choose wrist guards. However, there is nothing against wearing both. The professionals do. A pair of all-leather work gloves with a piece of foam rubber stuffed into the palm is good protection against abrasions.

Ankle Guards

Van's "Off-the-Wall," in the business of making athletic shoes, introduced the ankle guard. If you don't like your ankle bone getting hit by a runaway skateboard (and who does?), this is for you. The ankle guard also protects the tender Achilles tendon above the heel. Mr. Van Doren's son didn't like getting those bruises and told his dad so. Dad picked up some vinyl in the shop and his scissors and began cutting. When he finished, he had designed the Ankle Guard (after adding padding and velcro fasteners). It fits around any size ankle, is comfortable, lightweight, and protects.

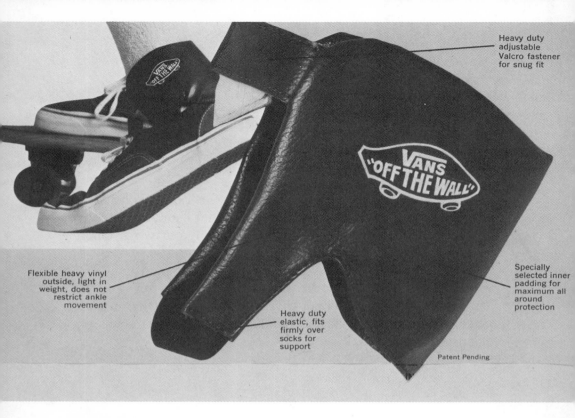

Heavy duty adjustable Valcro fastener for snug fit

Flexible heavy vinyl outside, light in weight, does not restrict ankle movement

Heavy duty elastic, fits firmly over socks for support

Specially selected inner padding for maximum all around protection

Patent Pending

The ankle guard protects the ankle bone from flying boards. *Courtesy of Van Doren Rubber Co.*

Shoes

Skateboarders must wear nonskid-sole shoes. Athletic shoes, or sneakers, are the best answer. Chose a style with a wide sole, not narrow as you would for track, because you want a lot of flat space. The more surface you have on the board, the better. Soft soles are preferable. They grip the skateboard. The closer a shoe feels, especially the sole, and as near to being like barefoot, the better.

High-top shoes are preferred for bowl riding. They give more protection and support to the ankles. The low-cut shoe is preferred for freestyling.

Shorts

Special skateboarder shorts with either built-in padding or insert pads protect against bruises to the thighs and buttocks and from injury to the tailbone. They are not bulky and fit well.

Style

Skateboarders are beginning to have a look that is distinctively theirs. Just as you recognize a football, basketball, baseball, or tennis player by the clothing worn, now you can recognize a skateboarder. Achieving this look began with the need for protection, as it did in all other sports. Color coordination followed, and then fashion.

The important point is that if you were going into any other sport, you—and your parents—would expect to be outfitted properly. Skateboarding should be no exception.

9
Mind and Body

We know skateboarding is a great outdoor sport. It's a challenge and a means of personal expression. You can enjoy it by yourself, in a group, or on a team. There is no pressure to compete, unless you choose to.

But Skateboarding Can Be Dangerous

Russ Howell, known all over the world as the King of Skateboarding, was asked this question: If you could say only one thing to skateboarders, what would it be? In his usual, straight-off-the-shoulder way, Russ answered, "Skate safe. It *hurts* not to."

Think

There are ways to protect yourself. Observing the safety rules and riding only when and where conditions are safe have already been discussed. Still another way to protect yourself from injury begins in your mind.

"Think about what you are doing," says Mike Cantu. Mike should know. He learned the hard way. He is a member of the Pepsi Professional Team. He rides the Pepsi Ramp and gives safety demonstrations. Mike had two bad accidents. One required stitches in his leg and the other was a broken ankle. Both

It looks so-o-o easy. Mike Cantu, a member of the professional Pepsi team, rides the big ramp for spectators. *Photo courtesy of 360 Sportswear*

times, he said, his mind was on something else. "One time," he said, "I was trying to think of what to say to my boss for being late. The other time, I was just daydreaming. Keep your mind on what you are doing," he repeats.

Your Body

The challenges of skatepark riding demand that you prepare your body to meet the action. Your muscles must be more flexible for skatepark riding than for many other sports or activities. They must be ready to reach and to stretch for that extra space the moment you need it. There are specific exercises for skateboarders.

The jump, bounce, and sweat type of exercises are *not* for skateboarders. Neither is weight lifting. These exercises tighten and shorten your muscles. You don't need great strength to skateboard. Three-year-olds can slalom and ride the bowls. But you do need to have loose muscles. You need to do a lot of exercises in stretching and twisting.

Curtis Hesselgrave, for years the foremost exponent of safety in skateboarding, advises *static stretch* exercises. Static stretch means holding the body in a stretch position for a count of 10 to 15 seconds.

When Dr. Frank W. Jobe, a famous orthopedist for professional football and tennis teams and a founding member of the American Orthopaedic Society for Sports Medicine, was asked what exercises skateboarders should do, he prescribed the same. "Static stretching exercises are particularly important for this sport. They keep ligaments and tendons more supple and also protect against hamstring pulls and groin pulls.''

What happens is that in skateboarding the muscles tend to tighten. If you are about to ''go for it'' on the lip or on the near vertical, your muscles need to stretch for that kind of action.

One of the common injuries in skateboarding is pulled tendons. Tendons are those tough cords which connect the muscles with the bone and cause the muscle to work. If the muscle is called upon to make the same movement over and over again in quick succession, it shortens. It will feel stiff. Therefore, when the tendon tries to pull the muscle into action, the tendon can be pulled off the bone. This can be more painful than a broken bone and the pain may last longer. It also can take longer to heal than a broken bone.

Static stretch exercises are specific simple *yoga* exercises. Do them each day whether you are riding that day or not. While you are doing the exercises, think about how they are helping your body physically and mentally. With relaxed muscles, no body tension builds up, more oxygen gets to the brain, and your mind works better.

Below are four exercises which will keep you limber. Don't rush through them. You are not trying to work up a sweat nor trying to become the jumping jack champion.

For the most benefit, first do each of the stretching exercises. Then repeat each one in rhythmic, slow-motion movements. This follow-up sets the rhythm for well-coordinated riding.

Your stretching is done in four directions: frontwards, backwards, sideways (right and left), and twisting.

Exercises

Frontward Stretch (to stretch the back)

1. Sit on the floor with your legs stretched straight out in front of you. Sit up straight.

2. Raise your arms above your head. Bend back 2 or 3 inches.

3. Come forward slowly, forehead aimed for the knees. Let your elbows bend outward and your upper body fall forward.

4. Take hold of your knees.
5. Pull to bring your forehead closer to your knees.
6. Hold for a count of 15.
7. Repeat two or three times, rhythmically.

8. As your body becomes more limber, graduate from holding the knees to the ankles. Don't strain.

Backward Stretch
1. Lie down flat on your back.
2. Bend your knees and bring your feet up against your buttocks.

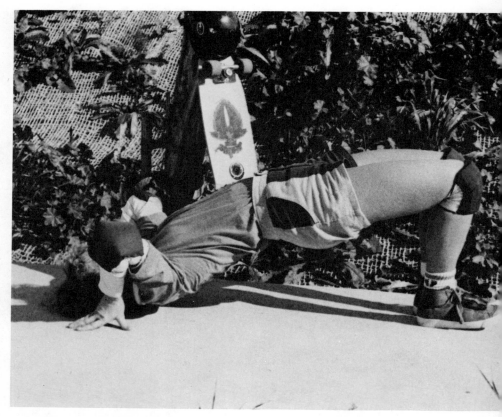

3. Place your hands on either side of your head, fingers point-ing straight back.

4. Arch your back.

5. Hold for a count of 10. Repeat two or three times, holding for a count of 10 each time.

Sideways Stretch (The Triangle)

1. Stand with legs about 2 feet apart. Raise arms to shoulder level, palms down.

2. Bend slowly to left, keeping your right arm outstretched and in line with the curve of your body.

3. Take hold of the left knee with your left hand. Keep your knees straight. Bring right arm over as far as possible without bending the elbow. Hold for a count of 15.

4. Slowly straighten to original position with arms outstretched.

5. Repeat same movements on right side. Hold for count of 15.

6. Gracefully return to original position. Lower arms, bringing legs together. Relax.

Twisting (The Yoga Simple Twist)

1. Sit on the floor, legs stretched out in front of you.

2. Cross right leg over the left. The bottom of the right foot is on the floor, beside the left knee.

3. Place right hand behind you.

4. Take hold of the left knee with your left hand. Your right knee is now behind the left elbow.

5. Slowly twist as far to the right as you can without its hurting. Hold for a count of 10. Turn forward and relax.

6. Twist to the right again. Hold for a count of 10. Turn forward and relax.

7. Do the same for the left side.

Use these same exercises to limber up at the park. It is especially important that you limber up before you go into competition. In this way you put your body in its best condition, and you can concentrate on what you are going to do.

10
Competitions

Competitions are fun and exciting for both contestants and spectators. There are competitions which have only one or two events such as freestyle or downhill racing and giant slalom. Others may have all these plus any number of or all of the following: broad jump, high jump, "bowling" (freestyling in the bowl), doubles, one-wheelers, tile riding, and pipe-pasting.

Kinds of Competitions

In general, there are two kinds of competitions: open and invitational. The open means that everyone may enter the qualification contests. Whoever qualifies progresses to the elimination, and on to the finals. The invitational means that all the

Competitions are fun and exciting for both contestants and spectators. *Photo by Glenn Miyoda. Courtesy of ISA*

contestants are invited by the competition sponsors. The merits of each can be argued. In invitational competition, all the contestants are champions. They may be, argue those who favor open competitions, but some unknown skateboarder may be able to outperform the champions. It has been known to happen.

Professional Versus Amateur

There are competitions for professionals only, for amateurs only, and for a mixture of professionals and amateurs (pro-am).

When do you cease to be an amateur and become a professional? A professional is one who has accepted not less than $100 for skateboarding. Receiving equipment, free riding time, clothing, traveling expenses, meals, or hotel accommodations when touring is not counted as cash. So these benefits do not classify you as a professional, nor does working as a skatepark monitor. You are a professional only when you are paid cash ($100 or more) for your skateboarding. A professional may be paid money and other benefits.

For instance, the members of the cast of *Skateboard Mania*, which toured the country, are professionals. Their costumes, as well as hotel and travel expenses, are paid for. They also receive an allowance each day from which they must buy their own meals. Besides these expenses, they are paid a weekly salary as long as they appear in the show.

Deanna Calkins, a member of the cast, says, "It's a good experience. Although, we put in a lot of hours—sometimes we practice 14 hours a day—it's fun. But I am also learning to take orders and do what I'm supposed to do. It's knowledge-expanding. I'm learning the discipline of staying in character. I love the make-up—it's like Halloween. Our costumes are beautiful, and they have full safety gear built into them. It's a good experience."

Deanna decided to become a professional because she felt that her skills had at last reached a professional level. She said that she has always liked the challenge of competing with someone just a bit better. "I worked up to it by entering amateur competitions."

Some champion skateboarders prefer to keep their amateur standing. They will not enter competitions which give cash prizes. Chris Foley, slalom champion, says he wants to continue riding for fun. "When they offer me a steady, weekly salary that will match, or exceed what I make at my present job," and he quoted a better than average figure, "then maybe I'll go pro." In

Chris Foley, amateur slalom champion, prefers to ride for fun. Skateboard World, Torrance, California. *Photo courtesy of Chris Foley*

the meantime, Chris continues to have fun while collecting beautiful Olympic-like medals and adding to his shelf full of trophies.

Competition—The Way It Should Be

Let's suppose that it's your first time to enter a competition. You saw the big poster in the skateboard shop weeks ago. The information flyers and entry blanks were right there where you could pick them up. You studied the flyer very carefully. You've heard that sometimes these events are run by guys who just want to take the sponsor's money, play the Big Official role, and disappear. They don't care if the events aren't run off in time and the skateboarders are still standing around waiting to compete after dark. You've also read about some pretty bad accidents happening. Irresponsible contest sponsors don't care if someone gets hurt. "That's what the public wants—excitement!" they say. Contests should have safety provisions and regulations for all events. And the material you picked up had all this information. So you decided to enter the competition.

Now that you're here, you're glad you sent in your entry blank and fee. It looks as if it's going to be just the way the flyer advertised. It said that the officials and judges would be champion and expert skateboarders—people who really know how to skateboard. You recognize several of them from their magazine pictures and a couple from the demonstrations you saw them give.

The flyer also stated exactly how each event would be judged, what penalties for which offenses, how to register an objection to a ruling—everything.

The line is getting long behind you. It was a good idea to get here well before check-in time. You're waiting to have your safety gear and skateboard inspected. The technical inspection is just like that given when you go to a really first-class skatepark. You must wear full safety gear. Your skateboard has to be in A-1 condition. Here they call it "Olympic Neatness." You bought new pads and wheels with money you earned working in the skatepark's snack shop. You pass inspection and receive a decal for your board to show it's passed inspection and a T-shirt with the sponsor's name on it. You're set. You feel good. Most of your friends are here. Some of them, like you, are entering both the slalom and the freestyling.

There are divisions for the competition: Girls, ages 9 to 12; Boys, ages 9 to 12; Junior Women, 13 to 17; Junior Men, 13 to 17; Senior Women, 18 to 26; and Senior Men, 18 to 26.

There are qualifying runs for the giant slalom. The five top racers will go on to the finals. After that event, there will be plenty of time to loosen up and practice for freestyling. A special practice area has been set aside for freestyle contestants. You've put together some special music on a cassette for your 2-minute freestyling routine. You brought two tapes, as the flyer said; in case one breaks, you can still go on. Your parents are here, and they are taking care of the tapes until you need them.

It's a good contest, you decide. The only thing that would make it perfect, you tell yourself, is for you to win a medal or a trophy.

The voice on the public address system announces that the qualification slalom runs for your division are about to begin.

Well, here goes. You can only do your best. And it's going to be fun.

11
Skateboard Associations

Equipment and clothing manufacturers, skatepark builders, owners, managers, competition promoters, or anyone who makes money from skateboarding *can* take advantage of skateboarders. Some have.

Skateboarders were sent to Europe to give exhibitions. They were given one-way tickets and were left stranded there.

Skateparks were being built by investors whose places of business were 2,000 miles away. As a result, they had no idea of what they were having built except something to give the kids a thrill with which to make a fast buck. They didn't seem to mind if their park rides also gave a "kid" a cracked skull.

There were local competitions where rules were made up while the contest was going on. With big prizes at stake, it was unfair to skateboarders. Little or no safety gear was provided or required. Downhill and slalom races were staged with the finish line only a few yards away from a busy intersection. There were severe injuries and deaths. Something needed to be done.

International Skateboard Association (ISA)

At about this time, responsible manufacturers were attracted to the work of Sally Anne Miller of Irvine, California. This energetic woman, a former nurse, had been instrumental in the design and construction of the free skateboard course in Irvine. She also had obtained approval for the city's new 4-acre skateboard park.

Sally Anne knew what was needed for skateboarders. When

Executive director of International Skateboard Association, Sally Anne Miller knew what skateboarders needed. *Photo courtesy of ISA*

the manufacturers asked her, she told them. They established the International Skateboard Association (ISA), and hired her to direct the organization. Their services are worldwide, and their goals are:

- Establish skateboarding as a recognized and accepted recreational and competitive sport
- Promote and teach safe skateboarding technique
- Sponsor and sanction correctly organized pro-am skateboard contests
- Provide information and consultation to the public and to members regarding all aspects of skateboarding
- Train skateboarders to serve as competent and professional teachers and judges
- Initiate research projects dealing with skateboard technology, safety, and teaching programs

ISA is a nonprofit organization. It is a center for information and promotion of skateboarding throughout the world. It has a public information library on skateboarding at the offices in Costa Mesa, California. It provides a consultation service for professional and amateur skateboarders. Anyone—cities, groups, or individuals—who wants information on how to build and run a mellow skatepark, or how to run a competition, can get information from ISA headquarters.

Skateboarders, both professional and amateur, use the center as an employment agency to get jobs as skatepark employees, contest judges, or members of a sponsoring demonstration team. If they have to sign contracts, their contracts are checked over by the legal staff of ISA. Everything is spelled out in advance so that all parties know what is expected of them. If a trip is involved, ISA sees to it that round-trip fare and all travel expenses are paid in advance by the sponsor. The skateboarders—amateur or professional—know they can phone Sally Anne collect from any place in the world if the arrangement is not working out properly. In return, if they don't do a good job for their employer or if they cause trouble, the least they can expect is a stern scolding by Sally Anne and, at worst, no more jobs.

Current sustaining members of ISA include top manufacturers in the skateboard industry and many of the most talented professional skaters. Associate memberships are available to manufacturers, publications, retailers, park owners, and others. General membership on both a professional and amateur level is also available.

Presently, ISA members are helping to create a national skateboard safety committee to establish voluntary safety standards for all skateboards and accessories in the country. ISA is also running an active amateur program.

For further information, write to International Skateboard Association, 711 West Seventeenth Street, Suite E-7, Costa Mesa, CA 92627.

New England Skateboard Association (NESA)

Not all of skateboarding organization activity is in California. The New England Skateboard Association is another. Their aims are:

- Help coordinate all scheduling of contest and exhibition plans, thus avoiding conflicts of dates and titles
- Educate both skaters and their communities through safety clinics
- Conduct periodic conferences for park managers and retail-

ers to foster growth in the business
- Publish a current list of skateparks and proposed projects through a newsletter to members
- Sponsor a yearly New England Skateboard Championship to help promote New England's best skaters

The organizer of the association is Bob Judd, who puts out their monthly publication with news of contests and of who is doing what in skateboarding in New England. For more information, write to: New England Skateboard Association, Box 851, Greenfield, MÁ 01301.

United States Amateur Skateboarding Association (USASA)

Although this organization is located in New York, it extends its activities nationwide. Its principal activity is to sponsor contests for amateurs. USASA has a monthly publication for members which announces upcoming events and reports on current and past developments. For further information, write to United States Amateur Skateboarding Association, 570 Wheeler Road, Hauppage, NY 11787.

The Skateboarder's Reputation

The few skateboarders who insist upon riding on busy streets or doing other reckless things have given the sport a bad name. Skateboarding can be dangerous, but the same is true of other sports. Here are the findings gathered by the National Consumer Products Safety Commission, and the number of injuries in the period from May 1977 to June 1978 as reported by the National Electronic Injury Surveillance System: There were only a third as many skateboarding injuries as there were those suffered in baseball or basketball. There were five times more injuries to bicyclers than to skateboarders.

These statistics do not take into account that there are probably many more skateboarders than there are baseball and basketball players. In 1978, there were an estimated 30 million skateboarders. Furthermore, it is safe to guess that skateboarders put as many hours into their sport as do athletes in the other sports.

As encouraging as these figures are, even one accident is bad, especially if it happens to you. Besides the pain and suffering and lost skateboarding time, skateboard accident figures seem to get printed in larger type than accident figures in other sports. But the point remains that *you* can do your part in making those figures as small as possible. Skateboarding can be the finest personal sport going. There are dreams of entering the Olympics some day.

12
Skateboarding Around the World

Are people skateboarding in London? In Paris?
Of course. Before the end of 1978, there were over 30 skateparks in England. France had an equal number of parks with 1/2 pipe, bowl, slalom, and snake runs. There are parks in Spain, Belgium, Switzerland, Australia, and Japan—which had one of the first. Just about every place where there is skateboarding—which means wherever there is concrete—there are skateparks.

Britain

If you were traveling in England, say on Derby Road, Lenton Abbey near Nottingham, you'd come upon the Malibu Dogbowl—a skatepark with a California accent. Stacy Peralta and other Santa Monica Dogtown riders have been there.

At Kettering there is the Skateside Stadium, an indoor skatepark with artificial trees to skate around among the full pipe, 1/2 pipes, pools with tile, and freestyle areas and a head-to-head slalom run.

If you went to Brighton by the sea, you would find the Barn Skatepark. It takes its name from an actual barn on the grounds.

In South Wales at Swansea, there is a fully equipped indoor park with snake runs, bowls, and tiled pool.

If you're in London and want to find a park, check the phone directory for *Skateboard Magazine*, 14 Rathbone Place, London W.1. Editor Bruce Sawford will be able to tell you the location of every park in England and in a good many other places in Europe.

Spain

Mr. Sawford will tell you of another Malibu skatepark in the south of Spain at Benidorm, Costa Blanca.

Switzerland

Want to skateboard in the Swiss Alps? You'll find parks in Berne, Zurich, Lausanne, and Geneva. Check with the Swiss Skateboard Association (SSA) for exact locations.

Belgium and Other European Cities

There is a Belgium Skateboard Association. Paris, France; Madrid, Spain; Rome, Italy—large cities (and small) have skateboard clubs and parks. However, some cities, even some countries, have laws against skateboarding on streets or sidewalks.

If you are in France, you will learn that skateboarding is called *la planche* (the board) *à roulettes* (with little wheels). It's fun in any language.

GLOSSARY

Achilles Tendon: A tendon located at the back of the heel.

Aerial. A skateboard trick during which most of the wheels are in the air.

Airborne. The act of doing an aerial.

Axle. The metal rod on which the wheels are attached.

Bank. Curved sides of a channel.

Bank Riding. Technique of riding on the banks.

Base Plate. Metal bolted to board to hold the truck.

Bearings. Ball bearings inside the cone of the wheel.

Board. Skateboard, the blank to which the hardware is attached.

Boinking. Technique of riding the sides of a 1/2 pipe and doing an aerial at each turn.

Blank. Board of a skateboard.

Bowl. One of the shapes in a skatepark in which skateboarders ride.

Bushings. A pad used as a shock absorber.

Carve. To make a straight run on a skateboard through curves without making a kick turn.

Chamfer. Bevelled edge, as of a skateboard wheel.

Clay Wheel. Formerly the composition of a wheel used for rink roller skating and later for skateboard wheels. Actual composition was plastic, paper, and finely ground walnut shells.

Coping. A special edge used at the top of swimming pools and pools in skateboard parks.

Crouch. A skateboarder's term for stooping closer to the board by spreading the knees.

Downhill. One type of race in skateboarding, meaning to race straight down a hill.

Drop-in. Technique of entering a bowl, pool, or 1/2 pipe vertically.

Freestyle. Skateboarding tricks and techniques. Freestyling. Doing the tricks. Freestyler. One who does the tricks.

Gear. Equipment, special clothing.

Gnarls. Lumps in the concrete.

Gnarley. Concrete having lumps.

Grinding. Technique of riding along the edge, or the coping, of a bowl on the skateboard axle.

Grip Tape. An adhesive tape with a rough surface used on the deck, or top, of a skateboard.

Kick Turn. Technique of turning the skateboard on the back wheels.

Kinks. Concrete with hard ridges within it.

Kinky. Concrete having kinks.

Lip. Top of a bowl.

Loose Bearings. Not sealed in as with precision bearings.

Mellow. Description of a run, ride, or a park meaning smooth, good.

Mogul. A speed bump made of a mound of concrete.

Nose Bumper. A plastic edging on the nose or front end of a skateboard.

Novice. A beginner.

Polyurethane. A special plastic of varying hardnesses, often referred to as urethane.

Pool. One of the shapes in a skatepark in which skateboarders ride; identical to a swimming pool.

Power. High speed, with thrust.

Precision Bearings. Sealed-in bearings.

Pro-Am. Professional-amateur.

Pro Shop. A shop selling skateboard equipment and apparel.

Radical. Riding expressively, riding verticals, sometimes called "rad" riding.

Reentry. Entering after having done an aerial out of the bowl, pipe, or pool without stopping.

Rim. The edge of the blank, or skateboard.

Rip. Outstanding riding through the skatepark, or through the particular ride.

Riser Pads. A pad used between the base plate and the blank as a shock absorber or for more height.

Roll-out. Coming out of a bowl over the lip.

Sealed Bearings. Bearings sealed in a cone; precision bearings.

Sharp. Abrupt, sudden.

Shock Absorbers. Pad, bushing, cushion made of rubber or vinyl.

Skatepark. A park built especially for skateboarders and roller skaters to ride and skate.

Skidplate. A piece of rubber or vinyl placed on the underside of the tail of the skateboard to protect it from rubbing against the concrete.

Slalom. A particular kind of downhill racing, riding between cones or gates. It is the same in skiing.

Spacer. Pad or bushing between base plate and the board.

Static Stretch. A particular type of exercising.

Terrain. The surface you skateboard on.

Transitions. Riding between different degrees of curves and between curves and level terrain.

Truck. Metal axle assembly.

Truck Protector. Strip of metal or hard plastic attached to board and truck.

Urethane. Slang for polyurethane.

Velcro. A kind of fastener.

Vertical. Straight up and down.

Vertical Drop-in. Entering down a vertical wall.

Weight. To concentrate your body weight onto the board. *Un*weight: to lighten your weight on the board.

Wired. Skateboard slang for doing a trick with ease and confidence; knowing how.

Yoga. Special kind of exercises originated in India.

YA
796.2
W433

Weir, LaVada

Advanced
skateboarding

DATE			

AUG 22 1980

Ⓡ THE BAKER & TAYLOR CO.

SUCCESSFUL
TIME
MANAGEMENT
FOR
HOSPITAL
ADMINISTRATORS

SUCCESSFUL TIME MANAGEMENT FOR HOSPITAL ADMINISTRATORS

MERRILL E. DOUGLASS
and
PHILLIP H. GOODWIN

A DIVISION OF AMERICAN MANAGEMENT ASSOCIATIONS

362.11
D737n

Library of Congress Cataloging in Publication Data
Douglass, Merrill E
  Successful time management for hospital administrators.
  Includes index.
  1. Hospitals—Administration.   2.   Time allocation.
I.   Goodwin, Phillip H., joint author.   II.   Title.
RA971.D68   362.1'1'068   79–55063
ISBN 0–8144–5602–2

First Printing

FOREWORD

In the early 1800s, an English clergyman by the name of Caleb Colton described time in the following way:

> Wisdom walks before it, opportunity with it and repentance behind it; he that has made time his friend will have little to fear from his enemies, but he that has made it his enemy will have little to hope from his friends.

The authors of this book repeatedly bear out Colton's words. They have constructed the most practical and useful book for hospital administrators that has been written to date. Time management has received widespread attention, both in conversations and in writings, and can be valuable to people of all professions. This book is aimed specifically at the hospital administrator. Its contents deal with the unique characteristics of hospital management by direct reference and liberal use of examples. The book's usability will extend beyond the walls of hospitals, however, as most of the methodologies can be adapted for use by others.

The most important contribution this book makes is that it deals with a highly complex, personal issue and dissects it into understandable terms. This is followed by suggested sound techniques the reader may use not only in everyday work but in everyday living.

JAMES D. HARVEY, F.A.C.H.A.
President, Hillcrest Medical Center

CONTENTS

1 Introduction   *1*

2 A Systematic Approach to Time   *11*

3 The Value of Objectives   *26*

4 Evaluating Priorities   *37*

5 Analyzing Time   *47*

6 Planning Your Time   *63*

7 Conquering Time Wasters   *76*

8 Working with Others   *98*

9 Time for You   *115*

10 Commitment and Success   *125*

   Index   *135*

1
INTRODUCTION

Bzzzzzzz!!

It's 5:00 A.M. Time to get up. Another day in the life of Charlie Miller, hospital administrator. The alarm insinuates its way into Charlie's consciousness. He begins to wake up. His first thought is how ironic it is that his day even starts with an interruption.

Charlie wakes up slowly. He stretches, rolls over twice, and wonders what would happen if he were sick instead. This is a mild form of procrastination that Charlie practices on most mornings. He puts off the inevitable start of another day.

After ten or fifteen minutes Charlie's mental functioning approaches normal. He begins to think about the day ahead. The first important concept that emerges is that it is Wednesday morning. Then the thoughts begin to flow:

"Let's see, Wednesday—oh, gosh, the *second* Wednesday of the month. The personnel committee meets today.

"Wish we could get that final report from our consultants. . . . Sure would like to have our wage and salary program approved

1

in one meeting instead of having to drag it out over a couple of months.

"At least I won't have to worry about eating breakfast at home, since this is a breakfast meeting. . . . Sure hope Nancy checked with Dietary to make sure that the meal service was scheduled. I don't know what I would do without her—she kind of runs this committee to start with.

"I'd better get there a few minutes early to catch the chairman so we can talk about expanding the Human Resources Department. . . . Better get moving if I'm going to get there. I've still got to get up and run—need to—I got rained out two days last week.

"God, it's still dark out. It's just not civilized to get up in the dark. Why did I ever decide to run two or three miles in the morning? I know why—that's the only time I can actually count on.

"Got to keep that personnel committee meeting moving this morning because the administrative staff meeting at 9:00 has a full agenda. It will be 11:00 for sure before we get out of that meeting, and I really need fifteen minutes between meetings to return a couple of those calls I didn't get to yesterday afternoon. I can't wait until 11:00 to do that. And I promised the VP of finance that I would review the first-run budgets with him before noon so he could make his dinner luncheon with the chairman of the finance committee.

"Speaking of noon, I'm sure glad the associate administrator is available to cover that medical mortality conference. I need the lunch hour today to get started on the performance evaluation for the director of nursing services. That thing is three weeks overdue now, and I've simply got to get to it. No need for two administrative representatives to be at the mortality conference anyway. . . . I should be able to get a draft of the evaluation knocked out by 1:15 or 1:30 P.M.

"I was going to make up Rotary today, but I guess it can wait until Friday. I have to make sure we keep that date open, though. If I can get that evaluation out of the way by 1:30 P.M., I can just make the City Commission hearing and fulfill my role as trustee of the Emergency Services Authority. . . . Boy! That takes a lot of time, but it is important for the community; and right now the project is at a critical stage.

"It's a good thing we are having the hospital council meeting at General—that's only ten minutes from downtown. I should be able to make it. Hope that agenda is short. I really need to be back at the hospital by 4:30. For three days now I've been promising the administrator for general services that I would give him some time. I know he usually doesn't ask unless he needs it.

"Let's see, that should get me home by 6:00 P.M. That way I can have dinner with the wife and kids before I go back to the hospital for the general staff meeting at 7:30. Election of officers tonight—I hope the meeting doesn't last all night, but it probably will. . . . I planned on doing some catch-up reading on the last three months' journals, and if I don't get to bed until 11:30 or so, it will be tough getting up in the morning to run.

"Wait a minute! I haven't even gotten up this morning yet. Got to back up and take things one step at a time."

Like most hospital administrators, Charlie has a full day ahead of him. Is it a typical day? That's a hard question to answer. For Charlie, the day is not particularly unusual. But not every day in the life of the average administrator would match Charlie's pattern. Few people start their regular day by getting up at 5:00 A.M. in order to run two or three miles. However, an increasing number of businesspeople are becoming acutely aware that physical and mental fitness go together. More and more hospital administrators are realizing that if they are to represent the health care field, they must become role models. This means keeping themselves physically fit. Maintaining physical fitness usually requires a certain amount of self-discipline and an investment of time.

Managing a hospital is a tough job, and it's getting tougher all the time. An increasing number of people are making greater and greater demands on the administrator. It is simply not possible to satisfy all these demands. Furthermore, many of the demands are conflicting. Satisfying one may mean not satisfying another. In spite of all this, the hospital administrator is expected to produce better results every year.

If you examine a day like the one Charlie is anticipating, you soon realize that it involves a series of priority and time allocation decisions. At the beginning of the day Charlie will probably focus on the known events—those things that are planned and scheduled. But what about the unforeseen events that inevitably occur in any day? In determining priorities and allocating time, administrators frequently focus on planned events, overlooking the adjustments that may be necessary to cope with unexpected events.

The issue of priorities raises a number of questions. For instance, how many events in an administrator's day should be foreseeable? How many should be controllable? By what process are the administrator's time commitments established? Measured against other pressing needs and requirements, which of those commitments that have been made—or will be made—carry the highest priority in terms of receiving the administrator's personal attention? In other words, which of the administrator's commitments will return maximum benefit to the hospital and produce maximum results for the administrator?

As Charlie lay in bed deliberating his day, he recognized the value of sending an associate administrator to the mortality conference in his place. Perhaps Charlie should also have thought about sending other people to similar functions. Often, administrators fall into habits in allocating their time and fail to consider such important questions as delegation. When this happens, the result is inevitably an increase in wasted time and greater frustration.

Charlie's daily scenario is also remarkable for what it does not contain. For instance, Charlie has given no thought to allocating time for thinking, doing necessary paperwork, developing his staff, and doing many other important tasks that he should be paying attention to. Why do all the journals sit at home for three months waiting to be read? Where in the course of any given day does the administrator take some time for planning a better allocation of time?

A typical pattern? Probably! An unchangeable situation? No. Stop a moment and ask yourself this question: "If I were to be paid today on the basis of the percentage of time I spent on matters that relate specifically to my primary job responsibilities, what percentage of my daily pay would I earn?" After giving that question some serious reflection and answering it honestly, you will probably come up with a second question: "How can I increase the time I allocate to my most important activities— the ones that will help me meet my responsibilities and promote the overall welfare of the hospital?" The response to that question is what this book is all about.

This book is designed to help you identify appropriate questions. It will also examine some of the issues raised by those questions. It will help you analyze the resulting information and find the best methods for improving your effectiveness in allocating your time.

Remember, however, that no book or technique can give you more time. Time is a paradox. It seems that you never have enough time, yet you have all the time there is. Your problem is not a shortage of time, but how you use the time available. This book will help you discover better ways to use that time in order to produce more satisfying results. For most hospital administrators, that will be a significant gain.

As you progress through the book, it will help to remember some of the special characteristics of time. For instance, time is considered an important resource. But it is different from other resources in that it cannot be conserved. It is impossible to "save time." The only thing you can do with time is spend it. When you say you are saving time, you usually mean that you will spend less time on some task, but this "saved" time cannot be banked or held for future spending. All time is current time. It must all be used now. Many administrators fail to appreciate this characteristic of time. They continue to look for ways to save time, only to find that hoped-for benefits never materialize.

Time is different from other resources in another sense. Most resources must be purchased. The more they cost, the more you value them. Time is free. All you need to do to receive your daily allotment of time is to wake up each morning. Because time is free, many administrators don't value it very much. Ask yourself this question: "If I had to buy my time, would I spend it very differently from the way I spend it now?"

Throughout this book we will be using the phrase "managing time." This phrase is somewhat misleading, since time cannot really be managed. Time is a constant. Time is. Time moves at the same rate regardless of who you are or what you are doing. Time is not influenced by your desires or decisions. When we talk about time management, we really mean self-management. The essence of managing time is managing yourself in such a way that you achieve better results in the time available.

Why be concerned with managing time better? To get more done. To get more done in less time. To gain more satisfaction. To gain more personal time. To get better results. In your profession, better results must be considered from both a short-term and a long-term perspective. In the short term, better results may mean keeping the hospital functioning smoothly. In the long run, however, better results will depend on planning for the development of a better organization.

Each hospital administrator has a different style, personality, philosophy, set of interests, and values. Therefore, this book will convey a different message to different readers. However, the book contains something for everyone, something that can help each reader make more effective use of his or her time. Some suggestions and techniques will be easy to implement. Others will require considerable study, commitment, and self-discipline. The techniques will be only as good as your willingness to use them and to adapt them to your situation. Adaptability, however, is one area where most hospital administrators seem to excel.

A modern hospital poses many management problems and challenges that do not exist in the average business organization. However, the management concepts that hospital administrators should use are similar to those that apply in industry.

The added dimension of a primarily service-based organization and of uncontrollable external influences simply creates a different and perhaps more substantial management challenge. None of the techniques discussed in this book can change the environment in which you work. But they can help you become more successful in dealing with that environment.

Many hospital administrators go through a mental scenario similar to Charlie Miller's when they begin their day. As they do, they gear themselves toward making the first critical time management decision of the day. If Charlie is a good time manager, chances are he will have three miles under his belt when he sits down at his breakfast meeting on time. If he is a poor time manager, there is a good possibility that he will go back to sleep and show up late for the meeting.

Regardless of how skillful you are in managing your time, this book can help you. By studying and applying the techniques outlined in the following chapters, you can build a more effective professional and personal life. Read this book and use it. The time you spend will be well invested.

To get started on the road to better time management, take the time management quiz at the end of the chapter. The questions are designed to help you identify your normal time use patterns. Circle the number that best indicates your usual practice. Be honest with yourself! This quiz will show you those areas where you are doing well or improving. It will also help you spot things that need attention. A few of the questions may not be applicable to your particular situation. For instance, if you do not have a secretary, question 12 will not apply to you. In such a case, circle NA to indicate that the question is not applicable.

The lower your score, the better. A good score is anything less than 70. The higher your score beyond 70, the more likely that there are improvements you should be making. Take this quiz again periodically to check your progress.

8

SUCCESSFUL TIME MANAGEMENT

Time Management Quiz
for Hospital Administrators

	ALWAYS, OR YES	USUALLY	SOMETIMES	RARELY	NEVER, OR NO	NOT APPLICABLE
1. Do you have a clearly defined list of objectives in writing?	1	2	3	4	5	NA
2. Have you recorded your actual time use within the past year?	1	2	3	4	5	NA
3. Do you write out your objectives and priorities each day?	1	2	3	4	5	NA
4. Do you spend time each day reviewing your daily objectives and priorities with your secretary or key subordinates?	1	2	3	4	5	NA
5. Can you find large blocks of uninterrupted time when you need them?	1	2	3	4	5	NA
6. Have you eliminated frequently recurring crises from your job?	1	2	3	4	5	NA
7. Do you refuse to answer the telephone when you are engaged in conversations with visitors?	1	2	3	4	5	NA
8. Do you plan and schedule your time on a weekly and daily basis?	1	2	3	4	5	NA
9. Do you use travel and waiting time productively?	1	2	3	4	5	NA
10. Do you delegate as much as you could to others?	1	2	3	4	5	NA
11. Do you prevent your subordinates from delegating their tasks and decisions upward to you?	1	2	3	4	5	NA
12. Do you utilize your secretary as well as you could?	1	2	3	4	5	NA
13. Do you take time each day to sit back and think about what you're doing and what you're trying to accomplish?	1	2	3	4	5	NA
14. Have you eliminated one time waster within the past week?	1	2	3	4	5	NA

	ALWAYS, OR YES	USUALLY	SOMETIMES	RARELY	NEVER, OR NO	NOT APPLICABLE
15. Do you feel really in control of your time and on top of your job?	1	2	3	4	5	NA
16. Are your desk and office well organized and free of clutter?	1	2	3	4	5	NA
17. Can you successfully cope with stress, tension, and anxiety?	1	2	3	4	5	NA
18. Have you successfully eliminated wasted time in meetings?	1	2	3	4	5	NA
19. Have you learned to conquer your tendency to procrastinate?	1	2	3	4	5	NA
20. Do you tackle tasks on the basis of importance and priority?	1	2	3	4	5	NA
21. Have you discussed time management problems with your subordinates within the past month?	1	2	3	4	5	NA
22. Do you resist the temptation to get directly involved in your subordinates' activities?	1	2	3	4	5	NA
23. Do you control your schedule so that other people do not waste their time waiting for you?	1	2	3	4	5	NA
24. Do you resist doing things for others that they probably could, and should, be doing for themselves?	1	2	3	4	5	NA
25. Are you reluctant to interrupt your subordinates, secretary, or colleagues unless it is really important and can't wait?	1	2	3	4	5	NA
26. Do you meet deadlines and finish all your tasks on time?	1	2	3	4	5	NA
27. Can you identify the few critical activities that account for the majority of results in your job?	1	2	3	4	5	NA
28. Have you been able to reduce the						

	ALWAYS, OR YES	USUALLY	SOMETIMES	RARELY	NEVER, OR NO	NOT APPLICABLE
amount of paperwork you do and/or the amount of time it consumes?	1	2	3	4	5	NA
29. Do you effectively control interruptions and drop-in visitors rather than allowing them to control you and your time?	1	2	3	4	5	NA
30. Are you better organized and accomplishing more than you were six months ago?	1	2	3	4	5	NA
31. Are you able to stay current on your reading?	1	2	3	4	5	NA
32. Have you stopped taking work home in the evenings and on weekends?	1	2	3	4	5	NA
33. Have you mastered the ability to say no whenever you should?	1	2	3	4	5	NA
34. Are you spending enough time training and developing subordinates?	1	2	3	4	5	NA
35. Do you feel that you have enough time for yourself—for recreation, study, community, or family activities?	1	2	3	4	5	NA

Total Score: Add up all circled numbers

2
A SYSTEMATIC APPROACH TO TIME

The first book about managing time appeared in 1958. Others soon followed. Today, the topic has been given widespread exposure through books, articles, tape cassettes, films, and newsletters. It seems as if everyone has suddenly become aware of the need to manage time.

Why the sudden awareness? Consider what has been happening to the hospital environment in the past 20 years. Advances in medical technology have produced a wide variety of new procedures and programs, including burn centers, renal dialysis, kidney transplants, cardiac catheterization, heart transplants, cardiac rehabilitation, nuclear medicine, and the growing field of microsurgery.

Legislative changes keep restricting the administrator's freedom of action and complicating the job. An administrator must now cope with EEOC, ERISA, OSHA, EPA, barrier-free laws, and many more regulatory programs that were unheard of 20 years ago.

Regulatory legislation has added to the financial burdens of a hospital. In addition, equipment costs, building costs, labor costs, and material costs have been rising steadily. As a result, health care costs have risen significantly. The increased cost of hospital care has resulted in a wave of consumer and legislative critics who increasingly demand a reduction in hospital costs. Cost containment is the by-word.

The net result is a very different environment for hospital administrators today. They are expected to obtain better results each year, expand programs, contain costs, and manage a hospital that continues to become increasingly complex. Every aspect of the administrator's job has changed. Every aspect but one, that is. The hospital administrator still has no more time available to handle these increased demands than he or she had in the past. Twenty years ago the administrator had 168 hours a week. Today he or she still has 168 hours each week. No wonder more administrators are focusing on how to use their time to good advantage!

CAN WE REALLY MANAGE TIME?

Not all the time problems faced by administrators are externally imposed and beyond control. Some are, some aren't. James McKay, author of the first book on time management, made an important observation that remains accurate today. He said, "If you're feeling a shortage of time in your job, it's a sign that your management skills are becoming obsolete."* Pogo said it too when he observed, "We has met the enemy, and he is us!"

Better time management, like charity, must begin at home. McKay's message is as true today as it was over 20 years ago. Why? Because the very term "time management" is misleading. Many administrators think of time as something that happens to them. Not true. Time is merely a convention. It is a convenient yardstick for measuring the flow of life, for indicating the transitions of living. Time can't be managed, certainly not in the usual meaning of the term. Time is a constant, a given. Time stands still for no one, and it cannot be changed. Time cares

* *The Management of Time* (Englewood Cliffs, N.J.: Prentice-Hall, 1958).

not who we are or what we're doing. Time transcends all of us.

Still, we persist in talking about our ability to manage time. Consider one of Peter Drucker's most famous quotations: "Time is our most precious resource, and until it is managed, nothing else can be managed." Most of us still approach the subject as if it were us against the clock. And because we do, we fail to focus on the things necessary to make improvements.

If time can't be managed, then we need to shift our focus. Time management means managing ourselves in such a way that we achieve the best possible results in the time available. McKay was right. We feel a shortage of time partly because we're not in control of ourselves.

HABITS AND TIME MANAGEMENT

A great deal of our difficulty in using time better can be traced to our habits. Much of our time is spent in habitual behavior. Some habits are easy to spot; others are obscure and consist of complex patterns. Even when we engage in unique tasks, we approach them in patterned ways.

Habits, by definition, are semiautomatic behaviors. Because they are almost automatic, most of us don't know what they are. Habitual behavior is below our awareness threshold. Until we find a way to lower that threshold, increasing our awareness level, we will never know for sure about our habits. Many of the exercises described in the chapter on analyzing time are intended, among other things, to uncover these habits.

How do our habits prevent us from using our time as well as we could? Consider one habit pattern often observed among hospital administrators during the first 30 minutes of the day. Here is a typical morning in Charlie's hospital:

Charlie arrives at 8:00. The first thing he does is get a cup of coffee. Then he visits with his colleagues while drinking the coffee. As he finishes the coffee he picks up the morning newspaper and browses through it for ten to fifteen minutes. It is now 8:45. Charlie has been in the hospital for nearly an hour, but he hasn't yet started to work.

This pattern is probably repeated in many hospital offices

every morning. "But wait a minute!" you say. "There's nothing wrong with drinking coffee—and talking with colleagues develops good interpersonal relations." All true. But let's examine the above scenario more closely.

There may be nothing wrong with coffee. But coffee is not drunk for its nutritive value. Coffee is a purely social drink. This means that most of the time, especially in the early morning, when people drink coffee they also talk with one another. What do they talk about? Early morning conversations over coffee tend to center on sports, weather, family activities, personal health, and similar topics. These conversations seldom concern work. And the newspaper isn't much better. We read the sports page, comics, classified ads, and perhaps the front page. Few of us could honestly say we learn something of real value from browsing through the morning paper.

As bad as it looks, this particular habit pattern leads to something worse. There is an old proverb that says, "As the first hour of the day goes, so goes the day." Many administrators waste their first hour, accomplishing little or nothing, and establishing a poor pattern for the balance of the day. Furthermore, they don't even realize what they're doing to themselves.

People often think of habits as harmful. But habits can be beneficial as well. If we had to consciously focus on every activity we did, life would become extremely complex, tedious, and even dangerous. William James, the noted psychologist, put it this way:

Habit is the flywheel of society, its most precious conserving agent. The great thing, then, is to make our nervous system our ally instead of our enemy. We must make automatic and habitual as early as possible, as many useful actions as we can, and guard against growing in ways that are disadvantageous as we guard against the plague. The more of the details of our daily life we can hand over to the effortless custody of automatism, the more our higher powers of mind will be set free for their proper work. There is no more miserable person than the one in whom nothing is habitual but indecision, and for whom the lighting of every cigar, the drinking of every cup, the time of rising and going to bed every day, and the beginning of every bit of work are subjects of deliberation. Half the time of such a man goes to deciding or regretting matters which ought to be so ingrained in him as practically not to exist for his conscious-. ness at all.*

Beneficial habits should be developed, and harmful habits should be changed. Undoubtedly, many of the habits associated with work behavior will not be good ones. That's one reason people are always running out of time. But a habit is a learned behavior—and anything that has been learned can be un-learned.

Habits are learned by performing a particular behavior over and over again in specific situations. Examples include the way in which you tie your shoes and brush your teeth. Do you usually tie the left shoe first or the right shoe first? Which side of your mouth do you normally brush first? Do you usually proceed in the same manner until you have finished brushing your teeth?

CHANGING HABITS SUCCESSFULLY

Habits are predominant response patterns. They are triggered by cues. For instance, in Charlie's morning behavior described earlier, simply walking into the office was a cue for Charlie to have coffee. He didn't have to think about it; he simply did it. Drinking coffee is his predominant response to arriving at the office. To change our habits, then, we must change our predominant response patterns.

The following five-step approach can help you learn to change your habits so you can begin using time more effectively.

1. *Identify the habit you want to change.* Begin by pinpointing the precise behaviors you wish to change—the behaviors that are now preventing you from using your time effectively. This will require analyzing many of your behaviors and the situations in which these behaviors occur. The more you know about what you do, when you do it, and why you do it, the

* "Making Habits Work for You," *Reader's Digest,* August 1967.

easier it will be for you to identify those habits that hamper your performance.

2. *Carefully define the new habit you wish to develop.* Write out the specific behaviors you wish to develop and the situations in which it will be most appropriate. Draw a line down a sheet of paper from top to bottom. On the left-hand side describe your current behavior. On the right-hand side describe the behavior you plan to adopt.

3. *Begin the new behavior as strongly as possible.* Tell everyone you can about the new habit you are going to develop. Set up a routine to go with your habit. Put signs in your office reminding you of the behavior you plan to adopt. In short, do everything you can to develop the strongest motivation possible for learning the new behavior.

4. *Never deviate from the behavior until the new habit is firmly established.* You will be tempted many times to do things in the old way. Resist these temptations. Some people rationalize deviations by saying, "Just this once won't matter." The truth is that each deviation matters a great deal. Every time you deviate you must start over again. The more times you attempt to start over, the harder it is to acquire the new habit.

5. *Use every opportunity to practice the new behavior.* No matter how strong your resolution to change, the new habit will not become yours until you actually use it. Seek out opportunities to practice the new behavior whenever you can. Arrange your schedule to use it more frequently than normal. Do everything you can to practice the new behavior as often as possible, and it will soon become a habit.

How long does it take to replace one habit with another habit? This, of course, depends on the individual and the nature of the habit to be changed. Many work-related habits can be successfully changed in three to seven weeks. In other words, if you consistently practice the new behavior for three to seven weeks, the new behavior will become your predominant response pattern. At that point, you have replaced the old habit with a new one.

Perhaps the greatest difficulty that arises in changing habits is practicing the new behavior consistently. Many administrators do the right things some of the time. A few do the right things most of the time. Almost none do the right things all the time. Part-time practice doesn't develop good habits. Only consistency and persistence develop the kind of habits that lead to good results.

Lack of consistency is often due to our failure to see things in a systematic manner. We tend to view events in a hopscotch, fragmented way. We often view our work in a similar manner. A better approach is to focus on the connections between the events and activities that fill our day. A systematic approach to how we use our time will help us develop better time habits. Such a system will also help us solidify small gains into larger gains.

A systematic approach to managing time includes six steps:

1. Analyzing time use—discovering what's happening now and what should be changed.
2. Clarifying objectives—establishing a basis for evaluating the best use of our time.
3. Setting priorities—focusing on the activities that are most valuable.
4. Planning time—making sure that our activities match our objectives.
5. Scheduling—arranging our day to get more done in less time.
6. Evaluating progress—determining if things are working out well.

Each of these steps will be discussed in detail in the chapters that follow.

ASSUMPTIONS ABOUT TIME

Changing habits is not easy. Part of the difficulty stems from the assumptions we make about the world around us. Not all our assumptions are consciously developed. Many are unconscious. But whether conscious or not, these assumptions guide our behavior.

In working with a variety of administrators over the years, we have discovered a number of assumptions that affect an administrator's ability to manage time. Below is a list of ten of these common assumptions. Test yourself. Do you believe the following statements are true or false? Be honest!

Test Your Assumptions   TRUE   FALSE

1. Most administrators are overworked because of the nature of their job.   ____   ____
2. Managing time better is essentially a matter of reducing the time spent on various activities.   ____   ____
3. Administrators deal with people, and because all people are important, administrators cannot establish priorities.   ____   ____
4. Most administrators could solve their time problems by working harder.   ____   ____
5. Administrators who concentrate on working efficiently are the most effective administrators.   ____   ____
6. Most of the ordinary day-to-day activities do not need to be planned, and most administrators could not plan for them anyway.   ____   ____
7. Finding the problems is easy; it is finding the solution that is difficult.   ____   ____
8. The busy and active administrators who work the hardest are the ones who get the best results.   ____   ____
9. Administrators who really try to control or manage their time will miss out on many unexpected opportunities.   ____   ____
10. Time management does not allow for spontaneous behavior; it is dull and mechanical rather than exciting.   ____   ____

As with many things, there are no absolute right or wrong responses to these statements. However, some answers are generally better than others when it comes to managing time well. Each of these assumptions affects your ability to manage your time. As you read through the discussion of the assumptions below, remember that the recommended responses are based on observations of many administrators.

For each stated assumption, you can probably find an exception to the rule. This only underscores the fact that there are no absolutes. However, you may find yourself looking for exceptions to rationalize your different responses to several of the statements. If so, you are probably suffering from "assumption allergy." Your assumptions keep getting in the way of your resolutions to do better. The result is that you continue in your same old time habits. Even worse, you may believe that your situation is unique and that there is no solution. Before giving up completely, why not consider changing some of your assumptions? By changing your assumptions, you may be able to develop new forms of behavior.

1. *Most administrators are overworked because of the nature of their job.* FALSE. It isn't the nature of the job, it's the nature of the administrator. Everyone is overworked from time to time. If this is a normal occurrence, however, something is wrong. That something is usually the administrator. Being overworked is often the result of failing to establish the proper priorities, spending too much time on routine details and trivia, having sloppy work habits, and dozens of similar deficiencies. The job seldom overworks the administrator, but administrators often overwork themselves.

SOLUTION: Take an arm's-length look at your job. What are you doing that does not need to be done or could be done by someone else? Do you have trouble saying no to people? How important is each of your activities? Do you need additional staff, or do you need new ways to work? Finding answers to these questions will get you moving in the right direction.

2. *Managing your time better is essentially a matter of reducing the time spent on various activities.* FALSE. Managing your time better involves spending an appropriate amount of time on each task. For some things, this means cutting down on the time involved. For others, it means increasing your time commitment. You probably will try to cut down on the time you spend attending meetings, handling reports and correspondence, and engaging in idle conversation. You probably will try to increase the time you spend planning, thinking, developing subordinates, and engaging in other important activities. Remem-

ber, you are spending all your time now. There isn't any more. So you must subtract time from some activities before you can add it to others.

SOLUTION: Look at all your activities. How important is each one in terms of what you are trying to accomplish? Where could you reduce the time you spend on a given task? Where should you increase your time commitment? Are there things you are not doing at all that you should be doing? Your activities should always be consistent with your objectives.

3. *Administrators deal with people, and because all people are important, administrators cannot establish priorities.* FALSE. All people may be important, but all the events people wish to involve you in are not equally important. Indeed, in terms of your job, not all people are equally important. Are there some people within your organization who have more influence than others? Do you really treat everyone equally? This is not to dismiss the value of individuals or to deny human dignity. Administrators who hide behind the assumption that all people are important are usually the ones who do not want to make the hard decisions. All people are important as human beings. However, the activities, demands, pressures, and problems presented by various people are not equally important.

SOLUTION: Learn to separate the person from the issue. Be patient, polite, tactful, and diplomatic, but be firm. Managing your time to accomplish important objectives sometimes requires making hard decisions about how to respond to particular people.

4. *Most administrators could solve their time problems by working harder.* FALSE. Working smarter always beats working harder. The admonition to work harder starts early in life. From childhood you are urged to keep trying, to try just a little bit harder, to remember that working hard leads to pleasant rewards. "If at first you don't succeed, try, try, again." The problem, of course, is not so simple. Sometimes working harder is the best way. However, many people never respond any other way. Perhaps there is a way to shorten the task, eliminate some steps, combine some parts, and still get more done. If you only work harder, you will never seek out ways to work easier. Doing

the wrong thing harder doesn't help. The people who believe that the way to get more done is simply to work harder are the ones who work long hours, constantly take work home, suffer from stress and tension, punish their bodies needlessly, and still do not obtain the results they desire.

SOLUTION: Work smarter, not harder. Try finding ways to reduce the number of tasks you do. Make the job easier or quicker. Analyze your work flow periodically to keep things running smoothly.

5. *Administrators who concentrate on working efficiently are the most effective administrators.* FALSE. Efficiency does not necessarily lead to effectiveness. This assumption frequently generates the most active disagreement among administrators. The problem lies in the tendency to equate efficiency with effectiveness. The two are very different.

Efficiency concerns the cost of doing something or the resources involved. It is commonly measured in such terms as money spent, materials consumed, or number of people required. To be efficient is to use the fewest resources for a given task. Effectiveness, on the other hand, refers to goal accomplishment. Either you reach your objective or you don't.

Efficiency sometimes is referred to as "cost-effectiveness," which only adds to the confusion. Cost-effectiveness usually is expressed as a ratio of costs to results, or inputs to outputs. If your goal is efficiency, then becoming more cost-effective is an appropriate term.

The primary problem, though, is of a different order. Having equated the terms, many people set out to become more efficient, in the belief that being more efficient will make them more effective. The result is that they become quite efficient at doing things that do not need to be done at all or that contribute very little to their objectives. As Peter Drucker observed, "Doing the right thing is more important than doing things right."

SOLUTION: Focus first on effectiveness, then on efficiency. Determine first what you should be doing. Then ask yourself how you could do it most efficiently. Do the right things right.

6. *Most of the ordinary day-to-day activities do not need to*

be planned, and most administrators could not plan for them anyway. FALSE. The ordinary day-to-day activities are the ones that need planning the most if you want to control your time. Many administrators maintain that their solution is unique. ("Others can plan their day, but it won't work for me.") Many administrators accept crises and confusion as part of their job description. Nonsense! Anything can be planned. Those random, unique, hectic days follow some kind of pattern. Some patterns may be harder to discover than others, but they do exist. Discover the patterns and you have the key for anticipating future events. This is excellent information for scheduling and planning your time. Failing to plan those mundane daily activities means settling for random direction. Whatever happens takes control of your time. To break this haphazard approach, you must plan.

SOLUTION: Keep a daily time record to help identify the patterns involved in your job. Then use this information in planning and scheduling every day. Remember, though, to leave room in your schedule for the unexpected. When you start to plan, put emphasis on early actions. As the morning goes, so goes the day.

7. *Finding the problems is easy; it is finding the solution that is difficult.* FALSE. Failing to identify the problem properly is perhaps the greatest obstacle to solving it. The temptation to jump in with a cure is a very strong one. The result is that you are often busy treating symptoms while the problem remains untouched. To understand fully the nature of the problem, you will probably have to obtain data. For instance, do not just say the telephone is a problem. Find out how many calls you receive—from whom, about what, at what times, for how long. With this approach you find that many problems carry with them the seeds of their own solution.

SOLUTION: Do not confuse symptoms and problems. Collect data to understand the exact nature of the problem. The solution then becomes much easier and is more likely to work well.

8. *The busy and active administrators who work the hardest are the ones who get the best results.* FALSE. Being busy and

active doesn't necessarily mean achieving results. This assumption is instilled early in life by parents and teachers who continually admonish children to "keep busy." It is reinforced later by supervisors who constantly seek ways to keep workers actively engaged. Few of us escape this "busyness" trap. Few of us are encouraged to spend more time thinking about what we are doing. Physical activity seems to be far more valued than mental activity. As a result, most of us jump right in and start "doing something" without spending adequate time thinking and planning. This is the kind of activity that usually leads nowhere. It consumes time but returns little in the way of significant accomplishments. Too much time is spent on low-value activities that contribute little or nothing to high-priority objectives.

SOLUTION: Spend some time each day thinking about your activities. How much does each of your activities contribute to your objectives? What other important activities should be added to your schedule? Thinking before acting usually leads to much better results.

9. *If you really try to control or manage your time, you will miss out on many unexpected opportunities.* FALSE. The truth is that you are more likely to miss out on opportunities because you don't manage your time and thus "don't have time" to pursue them. Good time management ensures that time is spent on the most important activities and wasted time is minimized. Good time management means decreasing the time spent on marginal activities and increasing the time devoted to important activities. Those administrators who can effectively control their time are in the best position to take advantage of unexpected opportunities.

SOLUTION: Take a look at your objectives and the way you use your time. Are your activities consistent with your objectives? How many opportunities have you missed because your time was mismanaged? Get control of your time and you will find more ways to take advantage of opportunities.

10. *The problem with time management is that it does not allow for spontaneous behavior; it is dull and mechanical*

rather than exciting. FALSE. People who manage their time well actually have more time available for pursuing new opportunities and for engaging in spontaneous activities. Furthermore, they do so without feeling guilty. The reason is rather simple. Manage your time well and you are almost certain to get at least the same results in less time. Hence you will have more time for other things you would like to do.

SOLUTION: Experiment a little. Begin to manage your time well and watch what happens to your opportunities for spontaneous behavior. You will probably find that your life becomes a great deal more exciting.

How did you score? Were all your responses in agreement with the general rule, or did you have some disagreements? Score yourself as follows:

9 or 10 correct answers	Excellent—you're on your way to becoming a first-class time user.
7 or 8 correct answers	Good—you're still in good shape, but you'd better review your assumptions.
0 to 6 correct answers	Poor—your assumptions are probably getting the best of your attempts to manage time better.

If most of your answers matched the preferred ones, you are managing your time reasonably well. You should have little difficulty improving your time management skills. But what if several of your responses disagreed with the general rule? There are two possibilities. You may be one of the exceptions to the rule. You will need to examine yourself, objectively and honestly, to determine if you really do manage your time well.

The second possibility is more likely. As noted earlier, you are probably suffering from "assumption allergy." You have some basic blocks to overcome in implementing better time management techniques. You may have to change some of your assumptions before you can change the way you spend your time.

One last thought. In order to change, you must want to change. Ask yourself if you sincerely want to improve the way you use your time. All the good advice in the world is of no value if you do not want to do better. And changing the way you use your time is largely a voluntary effort. You cannot force other people to use their time well. And no one can force you to use your time well. The "want to" must come from you.

3
THE
VALUE
OF
OBJECTIVES

Things don't happen by accident. Things happen because people make them happen. If you intend to make things happen, then, you must know exactly what those things are. In other words, you must define your objectives.

Most people don't think about objectives very much. They just respond, react, or sometimes overreact, to pressures from other people or things. But if you want to control your time and become more effective in using time, you must determine exactly what your objectives are—and you must keep them up to date.

Realize that as situations change, your objectives change. As objectives are achieved, new ones must be added. As your hospital grows and develops, different things become more or less important on your job. As you grow and develop, different things become more or less important in your life. Your objectives will change to reflect changes in your industry conditions as well as in your personal values, experiences, and aspirations.

If you don't set goals or objectives, you are likely to find yourself battered about by all kinds of outside pressures, going first in one direction, then in another. The question you must answer is this: "What is the best use of my time?" The answer requires that you know what your objectives are—what results you are trying to achieve.

THE BUILDING BLOCKS OF TIME MANAGEMENT

Objectives are the building blocks of better time management. In fact, it is almost impossible to make good use of your time without a set of well-clarified objectives. How can you evaluate whether one activity is a better use of your time than another activity if you cannot determine what the end result of all your activities should be? How can you set priorities until you first understand your objectives? In the words of Lewis Carroll, "When you don't know where you're going, any road may take you there." And as many hospital administrators have discovered over the last several years, when you don't know where you're going, you'll probably wind up somewhere else.

Objectives are also a very important element in maintaining personal stability. One poignant reminder of this occurred when Buzz Aldrin, one of the first astronauts to reach the moon, suffered an emotional collapse shortly after his return to earth. Aldrin spent some time in the hospital recovering from his breakdown. To many people, this was a mystery. "Why," they asked, "should this happen to Aldrin? Why him of all people?" To the outside observer, it seemed that Aldrin had everything going for him. And in many ways he did. Aldrin wrote a book about his experiences to answer the questions of puzzled observers. He said the reason for his mental collapse was simple. He simply forgot that there was life after the moon. He didn't have any further objectives. He found it virtually impossible to function in that kind of personal vacuum.

People tend to think of objectives in rather abstract terms. Good objectives are specific and concrete, not vague and ambiguous. Many administrators are not as successful as they could be because they fail to select and pursue specific objectives.

They shift from one activity to another without any focus or purpose. They naively assume that things will take care of themselves or will be taken care of by others.

How often should objectives be considered? Every day. How far into the future should objectives be projected? As far as possible. The further objectives are projected into the future, the easier it is to know what to do right now. For you individually, objectives might be projected for a lifetime. For your hospital, some objectives should certainly be projected several years into the future.

Objectives may be easier to understand if you think of them as forming a pyramid, as shown in Figure 1. Each set of objectives builds on the preceding one. Thus the accomplishment of daily objectives should lead to the accomplishment of weekly objectives; the accomplishment of weekly objectives should lead to the accomplishment of monthly objectives; and so on up to long-range objectives.

An example will help clarify the objectives pyramid. Suppose the following annual objective were established for Nursing Administration: "Develop, complete, or revise, and have approved 12 standards of nursing practice." This objective might be a reasonable attempt to provide standards of continuity in the way nursing procedures are carried out. In order to do that, the hospital must document the process, establish the levels of personnel required for the activities or procedures, and make this documentation available to nursing personnel. The admin-

Figure 1. The objectives pyramid.

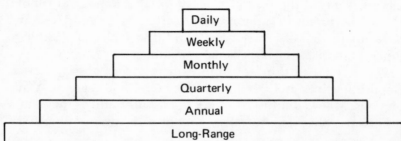

istrator with primary responsibility for nursing administration now has a well-clarified objective. By the end of the year, 12 standards of nursing practice should be approved and ready for use.

In using the objectives pyramid, the administrator would first break down the annual objective into quarterly objectives of three standards per quarter. Breaking this down further would yield one standard per month. Breaking this down into weekly units might yield the following subobjectives:

Week 1—determine top-priority standard for review.
Week 2—review and revise standard.
Week 3—review and approve revised standard.
Week 4—prepare final version of standard.

To make a weekly objective operative on a daily basis, the administrator would have to identify the steps necessary to accomplish the weekly objective and the activities to be done each day. Of course, the administrator may not have to take action every day during the week. However, action will be required on some days during the week if the weekly objective is to be met. Again, if weekly objectives are met, monthly objectives will be met; if monthly objectives are met, quarterly objectives will be met; and hence the annual objective will be met.

MBO AND ACTIVITY TRAPS

Many hospitals are beginning to consider the merit of management by objectives (MBO). While this book is not intended to explain MBO systems in hospitals, there is one point that should be clarified. In recent years many experts have noted that a large number of MBO systems are not as successful as they might be. One reason is that these systems fail to establish a connection between longer-range objectives and day-by-day living. Approaching objectives in a pyramidal fashion should help establish that connection.

"Activity traps" are another consideration in working to

achieve objectives. As George Odiorne notes in his book *Management and the Activity Trap,** an activity trap occurs when people become so engrossed in an activity that they lose sight of its purpose. People fall into activity traps in the absence of objectives. When people begin focusing on activities without relating them to longer-range objectives, a strange thing begins to happen. The activities take on meaning in and of themselves. The activities become more important than they ought to be. Why? Because people must focus on something. And if there is no objective, then people focus on activities. But this inversion of means and ends is not likely to produce the kind of results administrators desire.

Activity traps can occur even in an organization that supposedly manages by objectives. It's interesting to see how this develops. Suppose that an administrator begins to write an annual performance objective. Now we know that whenever a performance objective is written down, the probability of achieving it increases. But this result does not happen automatically. The administrator must still take action in order to achieve the objective. The question is: When does the administrator begin to take action? When does he or she become concerned about whether progress is being made toward the objective?

Before answering that question, let's consider a phenomenon familiar to all of us. This phenomenon usually appears early in life, certainly by the time a child attends school. If the child brings home a work assignment, when does he or she actually do it? The answer seems to be as late as possible—typically the night before the assignment is due. By the time the child leaves school, this pattern is well reinforced.

When does an administrator become concerned about the accomplishment of an annual objective? Toward the end of the year, of course. Becoming concerned toward the end of the year is certainly better than never becoming concerned at all. However, the more frequently the administrator becomes concerned, the more likely that he or she will acomplish the objective.

* New York: Harper & Row, 1974.

Suppose the administrator breaks down the annual objective into quarterly objectives. He or she will probably become concerned about the accomplishment of quarterly objectives toward the end of each quarter. But now the administrator is becoming concerned four times a year, not just once. If quarterly objectives are broken down into monthly objectives, the administrator will become concerned about the accomplishment of monthly objectives toward the end of the month. But now he or she is excited 12 times each year. If monthly objectives are broken down into weekly objectives, the administrator will become concerned about accomplishing objectives 52 times each year. And, accordingly, weekly objectives can be broken down into daily objectives. At this point, the administrator has discovered how to make long-range objectives operational on a daily basis. When will he or she become concerned about the daily objectives? Probably toward the latter part of the day. But when concern occurs this frequently, results are bound to follow.

By habit, most of us tend to put things off until deadlines approach. By breaking objectives down into subunits as small as days or weeks, we can make this habit work for us instead of against us. We don't change our habit; we simply change the structure of the deadlines. The old habit will work in the same fashion, but the results will now be beneficial instead of detrimental.

WRITING "GOOD" OBJECTIVES

Writing good objectives is not easy. A good objective is one that motivates you to take action and provides direction for that action. There are several criteria that can be used for writing good objectives. These criteria will help you improve your efforts and enable you to develop objectives that really work for you.

1. *Objectives should be your own.* You are more likely to work at and accomplish objectives that you set for yourself. This does not mean that you cannot accept an objective that your boss, friend, or spouse wants you to accomplish. But your

motivation will be higher if you consciously consider the advantages and disadvantages of a proposed course of action and then make your own decision. You should own at least some part of the objective. You should be willing to listen to and talk to others, but you should still do your own thinking and deciding. The more the objective is your own, the more you will be committed to its accomplishment. Within the hospital, this means that objectives should be jointly decided by superiors and subordinates. This applies at all levels of the organization.

2. *Objectives should be written.* Many administrators think that writing objectives is unnecessary. They prefer to keep their objectives "in their head" and feel that as long as they think about them it doesn't matter if the objectives are written down or not. This is a dangerous assumption. The purpose of writing objectives is to clarify them. There seems to be a special kind of magic in writing objectives. Once an objective is written down, your investment in it increases. As your investment increases, your personal commitment increases. Written objectives have other advantages too. They are less likely to be forgotten or lost in the midst of daily pressures. When objectives are written down, it is easier to integrate several objectives at once and to identify and resolve conflicts among them. If you are serious about using your time more effectively, you must write down your objectives.

3. *Objectives should be realistic and attainable.* If an objective is unrealistic, it is not an objective at all. Fantasies, daydreams, aspirations, and good intentions won't do. An object must be attainable. This doesn't mean that you should set your objectives low. Objectives should be challenging; they should make you stretch and grow. But they must also be set at a reasonable level—one toward which you are both able and willing to work. Although your motivation increases as your objectives get higher, if you set an objective so high that you don't believe you can accomplish it, you will probably never try.

Attainability is difficult to define. Ultimately, each person or organization must judge what is truly attainable. History is full of examples of people achieving "unattainable" objectives. If an objective feels right to you, and if it makes sense to you, it is probably within your reach. But do not become so optimistic that you set too many objectives to be accomplished in too short a time.

4. *Objectives should be specific and measurable.* When objectives are stated in vague terms, they provide very little direction. It is difficult to know exactly where to start and in what direction to proceed. For example, an administrator bothered with excessive turnover in the laundry might set this objective: "Reduce turnover of laundry personnel." While this may be an admirable intention, it is not nearly as good as if the administrator had stated: "Reduce turnover of laundry personnel by 40 percent within 12 months." The latter statement is specific and measurable.

If at all possible, quantify your objectives. Make every effort to find some way to measure them precisely. For example, suppose your objective is to improve the effectiveness of the relationship between your assistant administrator and the medical staff. A direct measure might be the number of unsolicited complaints or compliments received from medical staff persons. To measure the objective indirectly, randomly survey medical staff persons, and ask them to subjectively evaluate the assistant administrator's effectiveness in dealing with them. If you simply can't measure an objective directly or indirectly, you will have to exercise subjective judgment in determining your progress. Whenever possible, try to restate the objective in such a way that quantified measurement is possible.

5. *Objectives should have time schedules.* Assigning target dates for accomplishing objectives increases motivation, commitment, and action. Objectives without time schedules rapidly disintegrate into daydreams under the pressure of daily affairs. Each step along the way should be assigned a realistic target date that can, and should, be adjusted if conditions change. As each target date is reached, you will experience pride of accomplishment and greater confidence in your ability to achieve still higher objectives.

6. *Objectives should be compatible.* Your objectives should be compatible with one another. Otherwise, accomplishing one may prevent you from accomplishing another. For example, one objective might be to develop or expand the hospital's outreach program to the community—a worthwhile objective, but it will require additional expenditures. Another objective may be to reduce operating costs by 15 percent, which is also a worthwhile objective. It may be possible to achieve both objectives by reallocating resources within the overall budget. But it may be just as likely that both these objectives cannot be achieved simultaneously. Incompatible objectives frequently occur if different departments set their own objectives independently. Often, the hospital's objectives and those of an individual administrator may be incompatible. If objectives are incompatible, you may feel uncertain about which objective to pursue and may end up pursuing no objective at all. The best way to avoid this problem is to examine all your objectives and resolve any incompatibilities among them before you take action.

The more closely your objectives match these six criteria, the better they will be and the more they will help you add direction and purpose to your use of time. Remember that writing objectives is a skill. If you have difficulty writing objectives at first, keep at it. Your skill will improve with practice. Well-written objectives are essential to achieving results. If you don't clarify your objectives, how can you ever hope to attain them?

Even if your hospital is not using an MBO system, you can begin clarifying your objectives in order to make better use of your time. A good starting point is to write down your significant objectives for a 30-day period. Compare each objective with the six criteria to determine whether it is well written. Then, break each monthly objective into a set of weekly objectives. (See Figure 2.)

Now look at the first week of the month. Estimate how much time you will need to meet each weekly objective. When you have made an estimate for each objective, add up all the times to obtain the total time required each week to meet all your weekly objectives. Always estimate a minimum time for achiev-

Figure 2. Weekly schedule for achieving target objective.

OBJECTIVE FOR JANUARY 19XX
Conduct a survey within the central administrative offices to determine, through analysis of clerical jobs, how a central filing system
might change those jobs. Complete by January 31.
Week 1
1. Develop study outline—2 hours.
2. Introduce study and project leaders to office staff—2 hours.
3. Obtain support and prepare for data gathering—1 hour.
Week 2
1. Kickoff session for data gathering—1 hour.
2. Midweek check and review session—1½ hours.
3. Final collection meeting—½ hour.
Week 3
1. Summarize data—1 hour.
2. Analyze data—2½ hours.
3. Prepare preliminary findings—2 hours.
4. Review preliminary findings—1 hour.
Week 4
1. Prepare final report and recommendations—3 hours.
2. Review and accept report—2 hours.
3. Set objectives for February implementation—2 hours.

ing an objective. This does not mean that you will be able to
accomplish the objective within the minimal time, but it is a
starting point. Keep a record of your time estimates. They will
provide useful comparisons with exercises later in the book.

The importance of objectives cannot be overemphasized.
Consider this small example. A survey was conducted recently
to determine how word processing systems might change the
content of executive secretarial jobs. The survey team noted
that the average executive secretary spends approximately two
hours on routine typing each day and approximately six hours
on other items. A good word processing system should remove
almost all of the routine typing, thereby freeing the executive
secretary to use those two hours for more important activities.
However, the survey team noted that many of the organizations
that had implemented word processing systems failed to realize

the two-hour potential gain. It seems that whatever took six hours before word processing took eight hours after the word processing system was installed.

What happened? Parkinson came in when people were not looking. According to Parkinson's Law, "Work expands to fill the time available for its accomplishment." The survey team went further and questioned those organizations that failed to realize the two-hour potential gain. They discovered that these organizations also failed to do two other things: They did not clarify specific objectives for the use of those two hours and they did not engage in careful planning to make sure that those objectives were achieved. Again, when you don't know where you're going, you will probably wind up somewhere else.

4
EVALUATING PRIORITIES

Most of us have a fuzzy grip on priorities. We use the word "priority" to describe an important project or responsibility connected with our jobs. Under this definition, many of us would say that a small portion of our time is given over to our priorities. We would be correct in stating that it is simply not possible to always work on the basis of priorities.

The dictionary defines a "priority" as something given prior attention—in other words, something done before something else. This definition gets right to the heart of how administrators actually spend their time. Everything administrators do during the course of the day involves a priority decision. Unfortunately, many of these decisions are not made consciously; administrators are often unaware that decisions are being made. Nevertheless, the dozens of priority decisions made each day, whether consciously or unconsciously, go a long way toward determining what the entire administrative team considers to be important.

CRITERIA FOR ALLOCATING TIME

When we examine how administrators allocate their time, we find many complex answers. The average hospital administrator may be involved in 50 or 60 incidents every day. A study of priorities is a study of how the administrator decides to engage in any particular action at any particular time.

Administrators seem to use a wide variety of criteria in deciding how to use their time. The following list indicates much of the diversity. Administrators typically allocate their time according to:

1. Scheduled actions.
2. Deadlines.
3. Size of job.
4. Complexity of job.
5. Available resources.
6. Available time.
7. Consequences of not doing the task.
8. Whether or not the task can be postponed.
9. Demands of others (boss, peers, subordinates, family, friends, suppliers, regulatory agencies) .
10. What they like to do.
11. What they know how to do.
12. What's waiting.
13. Order of arrival.
14. Sequence of events.
15. Consequences to the group.
16. Planned events.
17. Intended results.
18. Political consequences.

Each of these criteria clearly has some merit in governing how administrators use their time. Certainly, no administrator can do exactly what he or she wants to do at all times. However, some of these criteria are more important than others for allocating time effectively.

Consider the demands of others. All "others" are certainly

not equal. Bosses seem to have a greater impact on how administrators use time than any other people in this category. Yet
not everything that the boss requests is of utmost importance;
nor should all things requested by the boss necessarily be done.
Nevertheless, many administrators respond automatically to requests from the boss—for a variety of reasons. Often the reason
is that the manner in which the administrator responds to the
boss's request plays a large part in determining future rewards
or punishments.

Let's take a typical example. Charlie is walking down the
hall of his hospital one day and notices that the wallpaper is
coming loose near one of the elevators. This section of the
hospital has been undergoing extensive renovation, and Charlie
is peeved that this eyesore has not been taken care of. When he
returns to his office, Charlie dictates a memo to his associate
administrator in charge of maintenance and repairs. When the
memo is received by the associate administrator, it will move
rapidly to the top of his activity list—whether it should or not.
Why will it be escalated? Because Charlie keeps a record of
how long it takes his associate administrator to respond to a
memo of this type. Charlie also makes a note of the kind of
response the memo receives. When it is time for him to conduct
a performance evaluation with his associate administrator,
Charlie retrieves all the memos and notes and discusses them
with his associate administrator even before he talks about the
associate's primary responsibilities.

Charlie believes that what he is doing is beneficial. He believes this because his predecessor thoroughly indoctrinated
him in the need to stay on top of details at all times. Charlie's
associate is learning the same lesson very well. Even though he
realizes that many of these memos are relatively unimportant,
he will respond to them promptly because he wants a favorable
evaluation from Charlie.

Consider the consequences. The associate administrator may
be doing his job very capably and may even have been aware of
the peeling paper. He may already have scheduled repairs in the
normal course of maintenance. The issue may have been
weighed relative to other needs and scheduled according to

some rational priority system. But when Charlie's memo arrives, this job is escalated to the top of the list. This means that while a relatively unimportant job is being taken care of, a more important job is delayed. Although this may be a good personal strategy for the associate administrator, enabling him to receive positive evaluations from Charlie, it is not necessarily a good strategy for the hospital. If there are too many of these incidents, the hospital may be in big trouble. At the very least, there will be more crises taking place than need be.

Charlie and his associate administrator need to find some rational way of dealing with such problems. This will require some understanding of how each one responds, and the kinds of things each responds to. It will also require some dialogue between Charlie and his associate administrator about the best way to utilize their time. Unfortunately, this kind of dialogue never takes place. It does not occur to Charlie to initiate the dialogue, and the associate administrator is too intimidated to do so.

Waiting until *deadlines* approach to begin working can also lead to trouble. The closer we get to a deadline, the more likely we are to engage in the kinds of activities necessary to meet the deadline. We rationalize this by saying that we do some of our best work under pressure. This is often true. Just as often, however, it is not true. Sometimes, the last-minute rush results in good performance, and sometimes it results in poor performance—or no performance. Deadlines are often missed. Administrators who tend to put things off until deadlines approach often find themselves working at a far more frantic pace than necessary. A better approach is to start well before the deadline, thereby ensuring more rational progress toward the goal.

Considering the *consequences of not doing a task* can be a useful allocation criterion. When tempted to engage in any activity, an administrator should stop for a moment and ask: "What are the consequences of doing it and what are the consequences of not doing it?" By taking a moment to consider the consequences, the administrator may change many of his or her actions. Things that truly have no consequence need not be done. Unfortunately, many administrators never ask this question at all, or don't ask it often enough.

Using *available time* as an allocation criterion usually just creates wasted time. Most people busy themselves with jobs that require relatively little time, putting off jobs that require large amounts of time. For example, administrators often tackle a lot of little things first to "get them out of the way," so they will have time to do the bigger things later. Of course, later may never come. This type of behavior is guaranteed to generate more crises than any administrator needs. Short jobs are not necessarily the most important jobs. It is better to work on important jobs in small pieces than to continue doing less important tasks simply because they are short.

Every job has parts that are enjoyable and parts that are not enjoyable. Many administrators do *what they like to do* much more readily than what they do not like to do. Unfortunately, not everything you enjoy doing is the most important thing to be done. Nor should things you like to do always take precedence over things you don't like to do. Some administrators have turned this situation around. If the disliked activities are more important, they do them first, at the beginning of the day, before allowing themselves the "luxury" of doing the things they enjoy most.

Order of arrival may work for a clerk in a shoe store, but it is a very poor strategy for an administrator who wants to be effective. Taking telephone calls in the order in which they are received, working on paper in the order in which it arrives, seeing visitors in the order in which they drop in, and similar habits will guarantee that you waste a great deal of time on trivial items. You must have some way of sorting out all these things so you can respond to the more important ones first.

Consider a routine that may sound all too familiar. Mary has been asked by her chief administrator to check over some personnel forms. As she starts the job, someone phones to ask about an overdue report. She gets out the file to check on the report but stops to glance at the mail at the same time. A letter on the top complaining about an admissions incident catches her eye.

She drops the report file, reads the letter, then starts for the admissions office to discuss the matter. On the way she passes the cafeteria, and the coffee smells so good she decides to interrupt her busy morning and have a cup of coffee. Her accomplishments so far: exactly nothing.

IMPORTANT VERSUS URGENT

Many unconscious priority decisions are based on a sense of urgency. Observers have noted that administrators are far more likely to engage in urgent actions than in actions that are simply important. The result, of course, is misfocused time. Whenever something important waits for something urgent but probably less important, the administrator is wasting time.

Years ago, General Eisenhower observed that there is an inverse relationship between importance and urgency. He told his staff officers that the more important an item was, the less likely it was to be urgent, and the more urgent an item was, the less likely it was to be really important. This seems to be a valid observation for hospital administrators as well.

Administrators always have enough time to do what is really important. The difficult part is knowing what is important. The answer requires some thoughtful analysis of the situation. It requires that we know where we are going and why, and how we plan to get there. Most administrators are too action-oriented to spend much time in thoughtful analysis. They prefer to be doing rather than thinking, and consequently seldom discover the right answer.

Many administrators live in constant tension between the urgent and the important. The problem is that important things seldom must be done today, or even this week. Important things are rarely urgent. Urgent things call for our attention, making endless demands of us, applying pressure every hour and every day. We seldom stop to question urgent things, never knowing for sure whether they are truly urgent or only masquerading as urgent. Indeed, many of the seemingly urgent tasks that fill our day are masqueraders. What we need is the wisdom, the courage, and the discipline to do the important things first. Only when we break the tyranny of the urgent can we solve the dilemma of the shortage of time.

The following exercise will help you analyze your situation and gain insight into important versus urgent activities. Begin by keeping a record of all your activities during the course of a day. Then ask yourself: "Why did I do that particular activity at that particular time?" Learning to focus on why you do each activity will help you understand which activities are important and which are merely urgent. Use the following matrix to analyze your activities:

IMPORTANT

		Yes	No
URGENT	Yes	1	3
	No	2	4

As you sort out your activities into the four categories shown, keep in mind the distinction between important and urgent. Important things are those that make a significant contribution toward your objectives. The greater the contribution, the more important the task. Important things also tend to have long-term consequences. Urgent things, by definition, have short-term consequences. Urgent things may or may not contribute to objectives. Recognize, too, that importance is a matter of degree. There is a continuum running between cells 1 and 3. At the one extreme are items that are very important; at the other extreme are items that are not important at all. Do not become too concerned about whether to place an item on one side of the line or the other. If you can't decide whether an item is truly important, place it on the "no" side—it probably isn't very important.

Let's consider the kinds of activities found in each cell of the matrix. Cell 1 includes those items that are both important and urgent. You probably spend a relatively small amount of time on these activities. Examples include a fire in the west wing of the hospital, a strike by the nursing staff, and the failure of a new addition to pass building inspection codes. Items in cell 1 tend to be identified as crises; most administrators prefer to have as few items in this category as possible. Whenever an item falls into cell 1, administrators have very little difficulty allocating time where it ought to be. However, in responding to cell 1 items, many administrators end up doing the right thing for the wrong reason. They ought to be doing something because it is important, but they are actually doing it because it is urgent.

Cell 2 includes items that are important but not urgent. This cell is characterized by things that aren't happening—or things that aren't happening often enough. For example, most administrators will admit that planning is very important, but few spend as much time planning as they ought to. Most administrators will admit that training and developing their staff is important, but few spend as much time developing subordinates as they ought to. Why not? Because making plans and developing subordinates are simply not urgent activities. They do not have to be done today, or tomorrow, or even next week or next month. They can be postponed, and they are postponed. But consider some of the consequences. The administrator who does not take the time to develop staff will have a less competent staff. He or she will also delegate less and do more detail work. The result will be one more overworked administrator with an underworked staff. Whose fault is it? The administrator's, of course.

If an administrator does not have enough time to handle items that are important but not urgent, then where is the administrator's time being spent? The answer is probably in cells 3 and 4.

Cell 3 includes items that are urgent but not very important. Most day-to-day, routine activities fall into this category. They include frequent interruptions and telephone calls, routine meetings and discussion groups, luncheons, traveling, and the myriad of activities that take up precious time but return very little. Unfortunately, not all these activities can be eliminated. Many of them can be minimized, but they still must be done. You cannot disconnect the telephone or stop seeing people. But neither can you allow the merely urgent things to govern your allocation of time.

Cell 4 includes items that are neither urgent nor important. Few people like to admit it, but cell 4 items occupy a very large part of their day. Indeed, observation indicates that items in cell 4 may occupy as much time as items in cell 1. Cell 4 activities include idle gossip, rap sessions, constant trips to the coffee machine, extra long lunch hours, straightening the papers on your desk, reading interesting but unimportant items in newspapers and magazines, and attending to little details that are part of someone else's job. Almost all these items could be eliminated. If less time were spent on items in cell 4, perhaps more time could be devoted to items in cell 2, which in turn would prevent some of these items from becoming cell 1 "crises."

PARETO'S PRINCIPLE

Another way to evaluate priorities is to follow Pareto's Principle. Vilfredo Pareto was a nineteenth-century economist who discovered that, in any given set of items, the critical elements usually constitute a minority of the set. Over the years this concept has become popularized as the 80–20 rule. According to this rule, "80 percent of the value comes from 20 percent of the items, while the remaining 20 percent of the value comes from 80 percent of the items." In other words, only a handful of things make a significant contribution; most things make little if any contribution. For example: Eighty percent of the patients in your hospital may be admitted by 20 percent of the physicians. Eighty percent of the crises may come from 20 percent of the departments. Eighty percent of your telephone calls may come from 20 percent of the callers. Eighty percent of your interruptions may come from 20 percent of the people who drop in. Eighty percent of your total expenses may be accounted for by 20 percent of your programs.

Carried to its logical conclusion, Pareto's Principle means that 80 percent of an administrator's results are accounted for by 20 percent of the administrator's activities. The question, of course, is what those critical 20 percent activities are. Many administrators simply don't know. They approach their job as if everything were equally important, as if everything simply had to be done. This is a "no win" strategy. First of all, there simply isn't enough time to do everything. Second, the strategy ignores the question of what is really important. Approaching a job as if everything were equally important leads to ineffective performance and wasted time.

Every activity you perform represents a priority decision, whether that decision is made consciously or unconsciously. The analytical techniques described in this chapter can help you evaluate what you do, when you do it, and why you do it. This information will give you valuable insight into the nature of the time problems you face and will help motivate you to make meaningful changes.

5
ANALYZING TIME

Many administrators are so accustomed to doing the things they do, day in and day out, that they do them without thinking. Countless studies have shown that many managers, including administrators, simply do not know where their time is spent. They cannot accurately describe what they have done or how long they have spent doing it.

Much of the failure to understand how our time is spent is due to the habitual nature of our activities. Because so much of our behavior is habitual, we often spend our days preoccupied. Preoccupation is another way of saying we have a low awareness of what's taking place around us. We observe very little of our relevant environment.

To manage our time well, we must have a very accurate understanding of what's going on—of what's happening and what isn't happening. Before we can begin to change our time habits, we must define what our current habits are. Too often administrators make changes with insufficient information. Changes made without enough information are very likely to be the wrong changes. Wrong changes simply compound the problem.

How do you currently spend your time? In order to discover

47

48   SUCCESSFUL TIME MANAGEMENT

your time allocation patterns, you will have to engage in some analysis and collect some data. This chapter will describe several approaches you can use to gain insight into your present time habits.

JOB FUNCTION ANALYSIS

Most administrative functions can be viewed from three perspectives: (1) what the administrator thinks he or she is doing, (2) what the administrator ought to be doing, and (3) what the administrator is actually doing. Examining all three perspectives will give you valuable insight into the nature of your job and will help you make sound decisions about how to reallocate your time to obtain better results.

Figure 3 illustrates a form you can use to perform a job function analysis. Begin your analysis by writing a brief description of what your job includes—what functions you perform within a typical week. How much does each function contribute to the objectives you are trying to achieve? How important is it? Then estimate what percentage of time you spend in each functional area during the course of a week. If you capture all your job functions, the column should total 100 percent.

Next, consider what isn't happening in your job. There are probably some things you ought to be doing that aren't getting done at all. If so, list those items as job functions and show their priority value. Then record a zero in the "estimated time" column to indicate that you aren't spending any time on those items at present.

When you have written down all your job functions and assigned them relative priorities and time estimates, review the items you have listed. Consider what percentage of time you should ideally spend on each item during the week. If you could really organize your job the way it should be, what would it look like? How might you allocate your time across these functions so that each received an appropriate amount of time? Record these ideal times in the third column. This column should also total 100 percent. In order to fill in the last column of the chart, you will have to complete the following exercise.

Figure 3. Job function analysis worksheet.

JOB FUNCTION	PRIORITY VALUE	ESTIMATED TIME (%)	IDEAL TIME (%)	ACTUAL TIME (%)
Totals		100%	100%	100%

DAILY TIME LOG

The cornerstone of your job function analysis is a time log—a record of how your time is actually spent. Most administrators have never kept a time log. However, keeping a log is not difficult once you know how.

A time log form is presented in Figure 4. Record your time in the following fashion. Enter your name, the day, and the date at the top of the form. Begin your record in the morning. Place the time log form on a clipboard and carry it with you throughout the day. Keeping the time log in front of you will remind you to keep recording.

Record your time in 15-minute segments. During one or more 15-minute segments you will be doing only one thing. For instance, you may be in a meeting for an hour. During other 15-minute segments you may be doing several things. For instance, you may receive two telephone calls, open your mail, and instruct your secretary. Do not be concerned about capturing every single event. Record the most important ones, or the ones that take the longest, and don't fret about the others. You will get enough detail for an accurate profile.

Record your activities as you are doing them throughout the day. Do not wait until the end of the day to write an item down. No one's memory is that good. Resist the temptation to generalize or to make yourself look good. You will be fooling only yourself, and the time invested in making the analysis will be wasted. Be as detailed as possible in your recording. Use abbreviations or codes if it is convenient and keep a record of what they mean. For instance:

9:45	TR dropped in to socialize
1:20	FM called about cost report
2:30	Dictated letters to BS, LR, and RT
3:15	Coffee

Each time you list an activity, circle the number indicating its importance. Remember that importance always depends on what you are trying to accomplish. The importance column should provide an overall picture of your effectiveness in using your time. You may also want to make a note of how urgent the event is and why you are doing it at that particular time. (Review the discussion of priority criteria in Chapter 4.)

List all interruptions in the columns provided. Indicate whether they were interruptions from incoming telephone calls or from some other source. Briefly note the nature of each interruption and who was involved. Record outgoing telephone calls in the activities column.

At the end of the day, summarize your recorded activities. Use the time record summary shown in Figure 5. Group activities according to the job functions you identified earlier. When you have completed your summary, transfer the information to the job analysis form (Figure 3).

ANALYZING THE RESULTS

You are now ready to analyze the differences, or variances, between what you think you are doing, what you ought to be doing, and what you are actually doing. You are ready to make the decisions necessary to take charge of your time and your job. You are ready to start making your time investment provide a better return.

Most administrators have never attempted to analyze their job systematically. The first time you try, you may encounter difficulties in developing appropriate classifications. For instance, should you lump all your meetings together regardless of their content, or should you divide them into categories? You should break things down into as many categories as necessary for the analysis to make sense to you. Don't become overly concerned with classifications or other details, however. Even an imperfect analysis can be very valuable. Many administrators find that this technique points out the true nature of their time problems better than any other approach they have tried.

One other point should be noted. Since you are spending all your time now, you will have to subtract before you can add. If

Figure 4. Daily time log.

NAME _____ DAY _____ DATE _____

TIME	ACTIVITY	IMPORTANCE	INTERRUPTIONS		
			TELE.	OTHER	NATURE
7:00		1 2 3 4 5			
		1 2 3 4 5			
7:30		1 2 3 4 5			
		1 2 3 4 5			
8:00		1 2 3 4 5			
		1 2 3 4 5			
8:30		1 2 3 4 5			
		1 2 3 4 5			
9:00		1 2 3 4 5			
		1 2 3 4 5			
9:30		1 2 3 4 5			
		1 2 3 4 5			
10:00		1 2 3 4 5			
		1 2 3 4 5			
10:30		1 2 3 4 5			
		1 2 3 4 5			
11:00		1 2 3 4 5			
		1 2 3 4 5			
11:30		1 2 3 4 5			
		1 2 3 4 5			
12:00		1 2 3 4 5			
		1 2 3 4 5			
12:30		1 2 3 4 5			
		1 2 3 4 5			

TIME	ACTIVITY	IMPORTANCE	INTERRUPTIONS		
			TELE.	OTHER	NATURE
1:00		1 2 3 4 5			
		1 2 3 4 5			
1:30		1 2 3 4 5			
		1 2 3 4 5			
2:00		1 2 3 4 5			
		1 2 3 4 5			
2:30		1 2 3 4 5			
		1 2 3 4 5			
3:00		1 2 3 4 5			
		1 2 3 4 5			
3:30		1 2 3 4 5			
		1 2 3 4 5			
4:00		1 2 3 4 5			
		1 2 3 4 5			
4:30		1 2 3 4 5			
		1 2 3 4 5			
5:00		1 2 3 4 5			
		1 2 3 4 5			
5:30		1 2 3 4 5			
		1 2 3 4 5			
6:00		1 2 3 4 5			
		1 2 3 4 5			
6:30		1 2 3 4 5			
		1 2 3 4 5			
7:00		1 2 3 4 5			
		1 2 3 4 5			

Figure 5. Time record summary.

ACTIVITY	TOTAL TIME	PERCENT OF TIME	COMMENTS

Figure 6. Sample job function analysis.

JOB FUNCTION	PRIORITY VALUE	ESTIMATED TIME (%)	IDEAL TIME (%)	ACTUAL TIME (%)
1. Guidance and direction to subordinates to ensure that sound administrative practices are carried out	*Primary*	10	20	30
2. Policy development and recommendations	*Primary*	10	10	5
3. Communication and coordination among primary managers	*Primary*	25	15	5
4. Problem identification and problem solving	*Primary*	25	15	10
5. Involvement with appropriate external agencies	Secondary	20	10	30
6. Basic support to facilitate subordinates' performance	Supportive	5	10	10
7. Staff support and coordination with board of trustees' activities	Secondary	5	10	10
8. Long-range planning and development	*Primary*	0	10	0
Totals		100%	100%	100%

you want to spend more time in one area, you will have to reduce the time you spend in some other area. This holds true of
your personal time as well as your work time. The adding and
subtracting sometimes cross the boundary between work and
personal time. All too often, hours are subtracted from personal
time in order to add them to work time. When this happens,
you begin to pay a higher price than you intended.

Figure 6 shows a completed job function analysis. The chart
indicates several potential problems. It suggests that the administrator may be overcontrolling subordinates, or perhaps has
too many inexperienced subordinates. It also suggests that the
administrator is being influenced too much by external agencies.

Some administrators may question the value of doing such an
analysis. Why is it necessary? Any job function analysis is done
for only one reason: to discover the discrepancy between objectives and activities. Although objectives are probably the single
most important aspect of good time management, you cannot
do an objective. An objective is an end result, something that
is accomplished. You must do activities. If you do the right
activities, you have a good chance of reaching your objective. If
you do the wrong activities, you may never reach your objective. Activities bridge the gap between where you are now and
where you want to be.

Many analyses have revealed that administrators engage in a
number of activities that simply do not relate to their objectives. Without some form of analysis, this situation may never
come to light and changes cannot be made. The discrepancy between activities and objectives is not intentional. It is simply
the result of how things develop.

In analyzing the results of your time log, ask yourself the following questions:

1. What went right today? Why?
2. What went wrong today? Why?
3. What time did you start on your top-priority task? Why?
   Could you have started earlier in the day?
4. What patterns and habits do you see in your time log?
   What tendencies?

5. Did you spend the first hour of your day well, doing important things?
6. What was the most productive period of your day? Why?
7. What was the least productive period of your day? Why?
8. Who or what accounted for most of your interruptions?
9. What were the reasons for the interruptions?
10. How might the interruptions be controlled, minimized, or eliminated?
11. What were your three biggest time wasters today?
12. What could you do to control your three biggest time wasters?
13. How much of your time was spent on high-value activity?
14. How much of your time was spent on low-value activity?
15. What did you do today that could have been eliminated?
16. What activities could you spend less time on and still obtain acceptable results?
17. What activities needed more time today?
18. What activities could be delegated? To whom?
19. Beginning tomorrow, what will you do to make better use of your time?

How long should you record your time? There is no set answer to this question. You should record your time until you believe that you have covered a representative period. For some administrators, this may be two or three days. For others, it may be two or three weeks. You should record your time at least once a year. Furthermore, whenever significant changes occur in your job, you should record a new time log. New conditions may require changes in job habits. A time log is the single best technique for gaining the information necessary to make intelligent changes.

Instead of recording the log yourself, you might have an observer follow you around all day and record what you do. A student administrative resident or an inexperienced assistant administrator might find the role of observer a valuable educational experience. The advantage here is that you will obtain a more objective record of your activities. The disadvantage is that you may be tempted to do things differently with an observer present.

Another alternative is to have an observer check on your activities at random intervals throughout the day. If you use the random-sampling technique, it will take approximately 30 observations per day for four to six weeks to obtain an accurate profile of your weekly time patterns.

OTHER USES FOR THE TIME LOG

There are several special time logs that may prove useful in helping you analyze your time. These include a telephone log, a visitor and interruption log, and a meeting log. Examples are shown in Figures 7, 8, and 9. These special logs provide more detailed information than is possible with a regular time log.

The time log is an invaluable diagnostic tool. In addition to recording how you spend your time, you can use the time log to match your activities with your objectives. To do this, you will need a list of your current performance objectives. Review all your objectives; then look at each item recorded on your time log and ask: "Which objective did this activity relate to?" You will probably discover that some activities are clearly related to your objectives, others are not related at all to your objectives. This is not unusual. Periodic use of the time log will help you reduce the number of activities that do not help you accomplish your objectives. As you discover nonproductive activities, eliminate them. Replace them with activities that lead to results.

You can also use the time log to determine who controls your time. Again, go through each activity listed and ask yourself whether it represents discretionary time on your part or time controlled by someone else. Caution must be exercised here, however. It is very easy to assert that someone else is in control when you actually have considerable discretion in performing the activity.

As you analyze the results of your time log, you are certain to receive some surprises. You may discover that you are very different from what you thought you were. You may be better

Figure 7. Telephone record.

TIME		IN	OUT	WHO	SUBJECT
BEG.	END				

Figure 8. Visitor and interruption record.

TIME		WHO	PURPOSE
BEG.	END		

Figure 9. Meeting record.

| TIME | | WHERE | | | EFFECTIVE | | |
BEG.	END	HELD	PURPOSE	WHO ATTENDED	YES	NO	WHY

in some ways and not so good in other ways. You may discover that you are wasting time in ways you never imagined. You will probably be amazed at how much time you spend in some areas and how little time you spend in other areas. All this information will help you verify exactly how you spend your time and will assist you in making wise decisions about using it better.

6
PLANNING YOUR TIME

Few hospital administrators spend as much time planning as they know they should. Yet planning is a critical activity if administrators are to spend their time effectively. Without planning, it is virtually impossible to match activities with objectives.

Because administrators fail to plan as well as they should, they are constantly bumping into Murphy's Laws:

1. Nothing is as simple as it seems.
2. Everything takes longer than it should.
3. If anything can go wrong, it will.

Administrators who spend an adequate amount of time planning run into these problems less often than administrators who don't.

WHY PLANNING IS SHORTCHANGED

If administrators don't spend as much time planning as they should, it isn't because they don't believe in planning. Ask any group of administrators if planning is an important part of their job, and they will tell you it is. Then ask them if they spend as much time planning as they ought to, and none of them will say they do. Why don't administrators spend more time planning? Ironically, many of them simply don't have enough time to plan. There are too many other things that must be done, and planning can—and does—wait for another day. It is very difficult to convince administrators that if they were to take more time to plan, they would gain more time for the other things too.

—Another reason many administrators fail to plan is that in the past they have been reasonably successful without planning. In the last 10 to 20 years, when economic conditions have been extremely favorable, many administrators have run up a series of impressive successes. Resources seemed to come from an ever-blooming tree. Many administrators were as successful personally as they ever hoped to be. And they accomplished all this without spending as much time planning as they thought they should. Clearly, some success was possible without planning. Whether or not these administrators could have been more successful if they had engaged in planning is a moot point.

The realities of today leave no choice for effective administrators. They *must* plan. Regulation and control from local, state, and federal government units demand it. The ability to develop new programs and services, keep up with the competition, finance operations, maximize reimbursements, and simply survive depends on careful planning.

Another reason administrators often put planning aside is that planning is simply not an urgent affair. In an earlier chapter we discussed the tendency for people to engage in urgent affairs before they attend to important affairs. Planning is one of those important things that is put off until the urgent things have been taken care of. Of course, by then it may be too late to plan.

Most administrators are action-oriented. They prefer to be in the thick of things, doing instead of thinking. As a result they adopt a reactive pattern—they react to whatever happens around them. Reacting requires very little prior thinking. To be truly effective, administrators must learn to *proact*—to initiate carefully planned action in order to achieve a specific goal. Proacting requires a great deal of prior thought and planning. This is difficult to do in a reactively patterned day. Therefore, most administrators continue to react, instead of carefully planning as many things as they could.

Many people pride themselves on being spontaneous. There seems to be a certain status attached to spontaneity. It's almost as though people believed that if they planned carefully they would miss the important things in life. This, of course, is nonsense. The more you plan, the more time you will have available for taking advantage of opportunities as they arise.

THE IMPORTANCE OF PLANNING

Some people view planning as an extremely complex, time-consuming activity. The task becomes so enormous in their minds that it prevents them from taking the first steps. Planning need not be a complex undertaking. Planning simply means thinking about the future in some systematic way. It means thinking about the things that should be happening and the conditions under which they should be happening.

It is useless to plan without knowing exactly what your objectives are. Therefore, until objectives are clarified, planning is impossible. Think of planning as bridging the gap between where you are now and where you hope to be. Where you are now is one side of the chasm; your objectives are the other side. Unless you can find some way to bridge the chasm, you will never be able to reach the other side. Planning helps you build that bridge.

Planning should include time schedules as well as activities. Tasks or activities are never ending. There is always something more that can be done. The limiting factor is time. There is never enough time to go around for all the things that could be done. Therefore, when a plan is constructed, it should be built around the most critical element: time.

Planning is the way in which you connect future points with today. It has often been noted that the further into the future you can project your objectives, the easier it is to know what to do today. But that future point does not have to be very far off in order to be of benefit. Most hospital administrators think one to two weeks in advance for most of the things that engage their time. The systematic approach to time planning presented here can easily be done within that time frame.

DEVELOPING A WEEKLY PLAN

You can learn to master time planning by approaching it on a weekly basis. Figure 10 illustrates a form you can use to begin the planning process. The key to successful planning is to do it consistently, every week. Plan those weeks that seem to be too simple to require planning as well as those weeks when you think you're going to be too busy to plan. If you plan your time consistently, every week, you will soon develop a habit of planning.

Once a week write down your objectives for the following week. Try to do this at the end of the preceding week. For instance, you might take time out on Friday afternoon or Saturday to make a note of your significant objectives for the coming week. These objectives should be well clarified before you proceed. (The process of clarifying objectives is discussed in Chapter 3.) Once you understand, as precisely as possible, your objectives for next week, you are ready to ask yourself six key planning questions:

1. What has to be done?
2. When should it be done?
3. Who should do it?
4. Where should it be done?
5. What priority should it have?
6. How much time will it require?

Remember, you cannot do an objective. An objective is a result achieved over time. You can only do activities. If you do the right activities, you have a good chance of reaching your objective. If you do the wrong activities, you will not reach your objective.

Figure 10. Weekly planning sheet.

WEEK BEGINNING_____

OBJECTIVES:
  1. _____
  2. _____
  3. _____

ACTIVITY	PRIORITY	TIME REQUIRED	WHICH DAY

– In order to determine *what* has to be done, you must focus on activities. Suppose, for instance, that one of your objectives is to have a new wage policy approved by the end of next week. In order to do this, you must think through all the activities you need to perform. If you perform these activities with a reasonable amount of skill, you should have an approved wage policy by the end of the week. If you do not perform the activities, the wage policy will not be approved by the end of the week. In that case, you will carry things over to the following week and fall behind.

– In answering the questions of *when* things should happen, keep in mind that there is a proper sequence of events. When things are done in the proper sequence, they take less time and lead to better results. If they are done out of sequence, they inevitably create wasted time.

– In answering the question of *who* should do something, think about what tasks you must do yourself and what tasks can be assigned to others. Delegation is an area where almost every administrator can improve. (See Chapter 8.)

– *Where* things are done can have a major impact on whether or not they are done effectively and efficiently. For instance, a discussion taking place in your office is subject to any number of interruptions. If the discussion were held in a conference room, interruptions would be minimized.

SETTING PRIORITIES

– Setting priorities among all your activities is mandatory. Plans will not always work out in the way they are written. When changes become necessary, always build them around the highest-priority items. If you fail to establish priorities, you may forget or omit some of the more important items in your rush to modify the plan.

Most of us are hopelessly optimistic about how long things take. We tend to estimate how much time it will take for us to complete an entire project. A better approach is to break the project down into separate activities and then estimate the time needed for each activity. You should always think in terms of minimum times in making your estimates. If you were able to work at a particular task without interruptions or distractions, how long would it take? This estimate should form the basis for your time plan.

Figure 11 shows a sample weekly time plan. The objectives are noted at the top. Activities necessary to accomplish these objectives are listed below. Next to each activity is a priority indication and an estimate of how much time the activity will take. There is also a notation of when the activity should take place. When the activity times are added up, the total for this example is 35 hours. Assuming that the hospital administrator will work an average 50 to 55 hours next week, this plan is already in trouble.

The trouble revolves around the amount of time that the administrator can hope to control. Observation indicates that the range of controllable time in an administrative job varies from 25 to 50 percent of the total time available. This means that an administrator working a 50-hour week can assume that 12 to 25 hours are within his or her control. If the administrator needs 35 hours to accomplish the objectives for next week, the weekly plan is clearly in jeopardy.

The problem with the plan shown in Figure 11 is that it leaves out several important considerations. For example, the plan allows no time for interruptions. It leaves no room for unexpected events or crises. It doesn't consider the impact of all those telephone calls and drop-in visitors—or requests by the boss. It does not account for the absence of staff members, changes in the weather, or other uncontrollable events. All of these things will happen. In spite of them, the administrator has a set of objectives to accomplish.

Whenever the time required to accomplish an objective is greater than the probable time available to accomplish it, something has to give. At first, the administrator will probably be tempted to say, "Well, they've all got to get done, so I'll just have to spend less time on each activity." However, if the minimal times listed in the plan are accurate, this is not a possibility. You simply can't do things in less time than they actually take. In addition, Murphy's Second Law reminds you that

Figure 11. Sample weekly plan.

WEEK BEGINNING   January 22

OBJECTIVES:

1. Complete preparation for personnel committee meeting on January 30.
2. Finish first draft of year-end performance report to the board.
3. Review final plans and cost estimates on nursing floor remodeling.

ACTIVITY	PRIORITY	TIME REQUIRED	WHICH DAY
1. Meet with personnel director to plan agenda	1	1 hour	Monday
2. Review format of year-end report with PR staff	3	1 hour	"
3. Brief accounting personnel on data display	2	1 hour	"
4. Complete reviews of all departmental year-end reports	1	3 hours	"
5. Review report and pension plan recommendations with actuaries for presentation to personnel committee	1	2 hours	Tuesday
6. Dictate first draft of year-end report	2	2 hours	"
7. Review presentation and approve final committee meeting agenda	3	1 hour	Wednesday
8. Edit first draft of year-end report	3	2 hours	"
9. Meet with director of nursing and assistant administrator for in-house session on remodeling	3	2 hours	"

Figure 11 (continued).

10. Meet with architects, director of nursing, and assistant administrator	1	8 hours (all day)	Thursday
11. Meet at bank with pension trust officers	1	3 hours	"
12. Brief chairman of personnel committee and personnel director	2	2 hours	Friday
13. Approve draft of year-end report for printer	2	1 hour	"
14. Handle any problems encountered in pursuing objectives	1	3 hours	"
15. Walk through area to be remodeled and visit with employees	1	3 hours	Saturday

things are not likely to be accomplished even within the estimated time.

Faced with this kind of difficulty, the administrator has several options. He or she could plan to do less than originally intended, rescheduling some activities for another week. Perhaps more things could be delegated. Or the administrator might work more hours than originally intended, utilize more staff than normal, or under certain conditions add temporary staff. If none of these options is feasible and the activities simply must be done, the administrator will have to find some way to create more available time.

At this point an important difference should be noted between having a plan and not having a plan. Let's assume that the administrator did not engage in weekly planning. When would the administrator be likely to discover that he or she had tackled more things than could actually be handled during the week? Probably Thursday afternoon or Friday morning. By

then, however, it would be too late to do much about it. The
purpose of thinking through the week and writing up a plan
is to discover potential problems far enough in advance to do
something about them.

The value of weekly planning cannot be overemphasized.
The weekly plan is the backbone of the administrator's strategy
for controlling time. Administrators who consistently prepare a
weekly plan always seem to get more accomplished than administrators who don't. Ironically, the fact that planners consistently
produce better results than nonplanners has not been sufficient
to cause more administrators to plan more often.

DAILY PLANNING

Once the weekly plan is completed, the next step
is daily planning. For most administrators this will take the
form of a "things to do" list. (See Figure 12.) Many administrators currently use a to-do list, but they have great difficulty
making the list work. The main reason is that administrators
often prepare their lists poorly. Most to-do lists are random col-
lections of activities, written down as they come to mind. Some
of those activities relate to objectives, but many do not. They
are simply random events that have appeared in the administrator's day. The lists may include everything from the most
important activities of the day to unimportant items, such as
"Buy a loaf of bread on the way home from the office." Very few
lists indicate priorities, and almost none includes estimates of
how long it will take to accomplish the tasks listed.

As a result, very few administrators are actually able to accomplish all the items on their to-do list by the end of the day.
They keep carrying things over to the next day, and the next.
Some lists grow to several pages long. And, of course, under
these circumstances administrators can rightfully say that preparing a to-do list seems to make very little difference in the results they obtain.

A to-do list prepared in this manner is actually demotivating,
guaranteeing the preparer a future of frustration. Because the
administrator seldom accomplishes all the items on the list, each

Figure 12. Daily planning sheet.

DATE _____

ACTIVITY	PRIORITY	TIME REQUIRED	DONE

new list is a frustrating reminder that the administrator is falling further and further behind. Once again, this simply supports the notion that writing things down has nothing to do with accomplishing them. To continue to write out a to-do list under these conditions is a futile gesture.

– A better approach is to base your daily to-do list on the weekly time plan. Each day, set out an appropriate portion of the week's activities. Begin by defining your intended objectives for the day; then write out your planned activities for accomplishing the day's objectives. Rate them according to priority and estimate the amount of time each one will take. You can then add other events that will occur in your day to the list.

Many of the activities on your list will not relate directly to your objectives. You will undoubtedly have to engage in most of them anyway. However, preparing a to-do list in this fashion allows you to compare important activities with unimportant activities. With things spelled out in black and white on a list, you may find it easier to let the unimportant things go until you have attended to the important things.

SCHEDULING YOUR ACTIVITIES

Once you have your plan for the day completed, you are ready to schedule your activities. Remember that things which are scheduled have a better chance of working out right than things which are not scheduled. The following guidelines — can help you become more adept at scheduling your time successfully:

1. Always put your schedule in writing. You can't possibly remember all the details of a hectic day.

2. As you schedule your activities, remember to focus on the objectives you are trying to accomplish.

3. Keep your schedule of activities in front of you at all times. Continually reviewing objectives, priorities, and scheduled actions will help keep you on track throughout the day.

4. Schedule around predetermined events. Block out all known meetings or similar commitments, unless you have the option of not participating.

5. Schedule early morning activities carefully. The way you start the morning sets a pattern for the entire day.

6. Group related activities whenever possible and do them in one block.

7. Don't hesitate to set aside large blocks of time for important tasks. Make yourself unavailable for some period of time during each day.

8. Allow enough time for each task, but not too much time.

9. Build in flexibility for the unexpected. You simply cannot anticipate or control everything. Until you determine the precise amount of flexibility needed in your schedule, leave at least 25 percent of the day completely unscheduled.

10. Include some "thinking" time for yourself every day.

11. Try to make waiting and travel time productive. Ask yourself what types of work activities you could do while waiting or traveling.

12. Learn to control your impulse to engage in unscheduled activities. If you don't, you will spend the day jumping from one thing to another and accomplishing very little.

13. Prepare tomorrow's schedule before you get to the office in the morning. Don't run the risk of beginning your day by reacting to whatever is happening before you've had a chance to consider what is really important.

14. Enlist your secretary's help in scheduling your time. You might even want to have your secretary schedule your time for you.

15. Keep a record of what actually happened during the day versus what you had scheduled. Comparing scheduled behavior with actual behavior will help you discover ways to become more effective in scheduling your time.

7
CONQUERING TIME WASTERS

—Clarifying your objectives, planning your time, and scheduling your daily activities are three giant steps toward gaining control of your time. But these steps alone are not sufficient. You must also take positive action to control the time wasters that threaten to destroy your plans. By improving your planning techniques on the one hand and eliminating many of your time wasters on the other, you take a double-barreled approach to getting on top of your job and using your time effectively.

Everyone wastes time. Even the best of us have wasted moments now and then. But there is a difference between the people who consistently produce good results and those who don't. The producers manage to hold their wasted time to a minimum.

IDENTIFYING TIME WASTERS

Exactly what is a time waster? There is no absolute definition. It all depends on your situation and what you're trying to accomplish with your time in the first place. You're wasting your time whenever you spend it on something less important when you could be spending it on something more important. Important activities are those that contribute to your objectives.

Unless you know your objectives, you can't accurately determine your time wasters. In fact, if you have no objectives, it really doesn't make any difference what you do—anything can occupy your time. It's when you have objectives, when you know what you want to accomplish, that wasting time is an important issue. What is a time waster to one person may not be a time waster to another.

All administrators waste some time. By their own admission, most administrators waste one to two hours every day. Furthermore, few administrators take the trouble to identify their time wasters. Of course, all of us occasionally recognize a time-wasting activity. We exclaim, "Boy, was that job a waste of time!" But even then we seldom analyze the situation carefully. Nor do we take positive steps to reduce or eliminate the time waster.

Even when we do try to identify our time wasters, we tend to be rather arbitrary. We jump to conclusions. Then we seek a simple solution for our snap judgments. There's a real danger here. Arbitrary, quick conclusions are not always accurate. More often than not, they are wrong. Time spent trying to solve the wrong problem is time wasted. We may even make the real problem worse.

A better approach is to systematically analyze our activities. How does each of them contribute to the objectives we are trying to accomplish? Which ones are a waste of time? Which ones are more important than others? This type of analysis can help us identify those things that truly waste our time.

A systematic approach to eliminating time wasters involves five steps:

1. *Identify probable causes.* Identify each of your time wasters and list its probable causes. Time wasters come from two general sources: (1) your environment—those things that other people do (or don't do) that end up wasting your time; and (2) your own shortcomings—those things you bring on yourself

that waste your time. It is easy to blame others for your time
wasters, but the culprit is frequently you. As you analyze the
probable causes of your time wasters, you will tend to shift from
looking outward to looking inward. You will realize that even
when others are wasting your time, much of the blame can be
traced to your actions and habits.

2. *Obtain good data.* Sometimes you will have to collect data
to understand the nature of a time waster. For instance, it's not
enough just to realize that telephone interruptions are a waste
of time. You need to know the nature of the interruptions—how
many calls you receive, from whom, at what times, about what,
and for how long. Good, objective data will uncover patterns
and help clarify the true causes of your time wasters. Sometimes,
you will need to obtain data to verify that what you think is a
time waster is actually where your time is being wasted. This
verification can best be done by keeping a time log, as described
in Chapter 5.

3. *Develop possible solutions.* Take each cause, one at a time,
and write down all the possible ways you might solve the problem. Many of the causes will carry the seeds of their own solution. If you can't think of solutions, ask others to help you. Be
as creative and innovative as you can when trying to solve your
time problems.

4. *Select the most feasible solution.* After listing all possible
solutions for each cause, evaluate each one. Which is best for
you, in your situation? Choose the solutions that are most likely
to be effective for you, and then develop your plan of action.

5. *Implement the solution.* When you find the best solution
to each time waster, take action now. Nothing will happen until
you act, and act in a positive manner. Be sure to evaluate your
progress. Is the solution working? Don't be afraid to modify
your plan and take another approach if necessary.

Of all the time wasters encountered by administrators, there
are about a dozen that seem to plague administrators most. The
following time wasters account for at least 80 percent of the
average administrator's wasted time. Read over the list and pick
out your top three time wasters. Rank them first, second, and
third. If some of your top time wasters are not included, add

them to the list. When you begin to develop your time management action plan later in this book, be sure to look back at your top three time wasters.

1. Interruptions—drop-in visitors, distractions, telephone calls. ‾
2. Getting involved in too much detail.‾
3. Crises, emergencies, firefighting.
4. Lack of objectives or priorities. ‾
5. Meetings.
6. Paperwork—memos, mail, reports, reading.
7. Leaving tasks unfinished; jumping from one task to another.
8. Attempting too much at once.
9. Indecision and procrastination.‾
10. Cluttered desk or office; general disorder.
11. Failure to do first things first.
12. Travel, waiting, commuting.
13. Routine and trivia.

The following discussion will offer comments, tips, and suggestions on how you can start controlling these time wasters.

INTERRUPTIONS—DROP-IN VISITORS, DISTRACTIONS, TELEPHONE CALLS

Interruptions are a part of your job. You can't eliminate them all, and you wouldn't want to even if you could. But you can manage your interruptions better. The secret lies in learning to control the controllable and to accept the uncontrollable. The frustration that comes with interruptions is often due to your attitude. If you work on changing your attitude, you can reduce the frustration you feel.

One of the major reasons drop-in visitors are a problem is that many administrators do not understand what an "open door" policy really means. An open-door policy doesn't mean that you are literally at the beck and call of anyone who walks through your door. To allow others to constantly control how

you spend your time is a sure way to get very little accomplished. An open-door policy means that you are readily accessi-
ble to those who really need you. This philosophy can be easily
implemented even if your office door is closed.

To get more done, you should modify your open-door policy
by closing your door occasionally. Establish a regular quiet
hour when you will not be disturbed. A quiet hour is a period
of uninterrupted time for concentrating on an important task.
You can create a quiet hour for yourself by eliminating seven
things:

1. No telephone calls.
2. No paging.
3. No unnecessary talking.
4. No excessive movement.
5. No interruptions.
6. No distractions.
7. No visitors.

No hospital administrator who really wants to institute a
quiet hour should have any difficulty doing so. It is an easy policy to implement, even in the most hectic hospital. But don't
abuse it. This means that you must make certain that you are
available to those who need you during other periods of the
day. Schedule regular times to see key people and staff members. Remember, much of the drop-in visitor problem is
created by your own staff. They may pop in on you whenever
they have a question because they don't know for sure when
they'll see you again. Have staff members save up items for your
attention and go over them at one time during the day. Do this
yourself too, so that you are not creating constant interruptions
for your staff.

In handling other drop-in visitors, remember this principle:
If the visitor never gets in, you won't have such a big problem.
There are a number of ways you can discourage the time-consuming visitor. Move your desk so you don't face the flow of
traffic. Remove extra chairs from your office. Try intercepting

people outside your office; you'll probably spend less time with them and still learn what you need to know. Remain standing so conversations won't last as long. When someone pops in to ask if you've "got a minute or two," say no and suggest a better time for talking.

Remember, too, that if you can keep interruptions short, you'll solve half the problem. Set time limits at the beginning of visits. Have your secretary interrupt you with a prearranged signal. Learn to be candid with people. Go to the other person's office—it is easier to control the length of the visit that way. Don't contribute to small talk yourself. Get to the point and end the visit.

—Ask any group of administrators about time wasters, and they'll say that the telephone is one of their top three. If only it wouldn't ring so often. Many administrators lament their inability to reduce social chit-chat or to terminate calls, their fear of offending callers, and their general lack of knowledge about how to control the telephones in their lives.

—To gain control of your telephone, you should develop a plan for screening, delegating, and consolidating calls. Many of your calls can probably be handled by your secretary. If necessary, delegate more authority to your secretary in this area.

Socializing helps make pleasant relationships. Recognize, however, that unnecessary socializing may stem from certain insecurities—the fear of missing something, a desire to be liked —and even from procrastination. Begin to sort out your motives and recognize them for what they are. Socializing can be reduced without becoming antisocial.

—Plan your calls. Prepare a short agenda for each call and have all the information at hand. Organize yourself so that you are ready to talk before you place the call. When your caller answers, get right to the point and stay there. When you have finished, end the call quickly, courteously, and firmly.

—Establish specific times for taking calls. Many callers will respect this system and call during specified times. Experiment with different times for different groups of people until you find the most appropriate schedule. Group outgoing calls for greater efficiency. It takes less time to place seven or eight calls if you do them all at the same time than if you do them throughout the day. Set a definite time limit for each call.

Tell long-winded callers that you have another call, an appointment, or an emergency. If necessary, hang up on a nuisance caller—while you're talking, not while the other person is talking. The caller will think you were somehow cut off and may not call back. Don't worry about offending people by being brief. Most people are not as easily offended as you think. Be firm without being rude.

Many administrators have established an answer-your-own-telephone policy. This egalitarian approach may be admirable, but it still wastes a great deal of time. The higher an administrator is in the organization, the greater the cost of that wasted time. Remember, though, that if others are to answer your telephone, they must be properly trained. You must work with them so they understand what questions to ask, how to ask them, when and how to refer callers, and what questions to answer themselves. You might call your telephone company for some free help in this area.

GETTING INVOLVED IN TOO MUCH DETAIL

One of the major reasons many administrators get involved in too much detail is that they tend to carry parts of their former job with them when they are promoted. If you find yourself involved in excessive detail work, your time log can help you analyze the situation. Review all the activities listed in your log and ask yourself: "Should this activity be done at all?" If the answer is no, discontinue the activity at once. Then ask yourself: "Should this activity be done by me or should it be done by someone else?" Answering this question can help you sort out those parts of your job that should belong to subordinates.

If you are a poor delegator, you will inevitably be involved in too much detail. Failure to delegate effectively stems from many different causes, most of them psychological. Your self-image, your self-confidence, and your sense of security have a tremendous impact on your ability to delegate. Following is a list of the 20 most common reasons for unsuccessful delegation:

1. Lack of agreement on the specifics of the delegated task.
2. Lack of performance standards and guidelines.
3. Inadequate training.
4. Lack of understanding of organizational objectives.
5. Lack of confidence in a subordinate's capabilities.
6. Lack of confidence in yourself; unwillingness to take risks.
7. Fear that a subordinate will perform better.
8. Fear of punitive action by superiors.
9. Interference by superior's superior.
10. Interference by superior.
11. Failure to understand the advantages of delegation.
12. Preferring to do a particular job yourself.
13. Mistaken belief that you are delegating when you are actually just assigning work.
14. Desire for perfection.
15. Belief that things are going well enough as they are.
16. Ambiguous understanding of job responsibilities.
17. Failure to establish adequate follow-up procedures.
18. Fear of criticism.
19. Unwillingness to allow mistakes.
20. Desire to be "liked" by subordinates.

Chapter 8 will delve into delegation in much more detail. Effective delegation is not only one of the best time management concepts; it is also one of the best ways to motivate and develop subordinates.

CRISES, EMERGENCIES, FIREFIGHTING

Most administrators believe that crises are an unavoidable part of their job. That's only partly true. Some crises are unavoidable. But the majority are either recurring crises or crises brought on by something you did or did not do. Whenever you're wasting time, you're probably setting up some crisis for yourself. When you put off that task you really don't want to do, you almost guarantee that it will become a crisis at some point.

Categorize your crises. How many of them are really unique? How many are recurring? How many are your fault? Get data about your crises. Look for patterns. Anticipate problems. Develop contingency plans. Expect the unexpected. Learn to react appropriately. Don't go into a "crisis mode" unless it really is a crisis. Keep your cool. Conquer your tendency to procrastinate. Learn to do it now. Stop putting things off until the last minute.

Start on projects earlier than you normally do. Give yourself more time to do it right in the first place and you will spend less time having to do it over. Pay attention to the amount of lead time you need to complete a project. Don't ignore deadlines. Discuss priorities with subordinates and superiors. Check with subordinates, peers, superiors, and others to spot problems that may be brewing.

When a crisis does strike, relax for a few minutes before tackling it. Prepare yourself for peak performance. And remember to practice good time management in the midst of the crisis. Don't start a second fire while trying to put out the first.

Of course, some crises are caused by events not under your control. Your boss may set unrealistic schedules or switch priorities at the last minute. Machines break down, people make mistakes, information gets distorted or delayed. Learn to live with these problems and stop fretting about them. Try to get other people to change their behavior whenever possible. Solve the recurring crises so you will have more time to handle the one-of-a-kind crises. But don't expect your job ever to be free of crises.

When a one-of-a-kind crisis occurs, try to learn from it. Turn it into an opportunity to test out new ideas, develop new procedures, or find better ways of doing things. A few crises may be just the impetus you need to make improvements.

Most crises arise from a failure to use time effectively. Change your time habits and you will probably notice a decrease in the number of crises in your office. Do a better job of planning, and things will begin to work out better. Take time to properly train and develop your people, and they will probably perform better.

LACK OF OBJECTIVES OR PRIORITIES

Failure to clarify objectives and priorities and to plan for their accomplishment is a leading cause of wasted time and poor results. Many administrators fail to set objectives and priorities simply because they are not in the habit of doing so. Often they were trained by administrators who also did not set objectives or priorities. As a result, they do not realize the importance of doing so.

If you have not set objectives regularly in the past, you will need to change your work habits. This will require developing some self-discipline. Try setting objectives and priorities for a month. Start with simple objectives. Spend a few minutes planning every day. Set down deadlines or target dates. At the end of the month, evaluate the results. This may be all you need to convince yourself of the value of continuing this activity.

Some administrators complain that there isn't enough time to plan. Planning—setting objectives and priorities—does take time on the front end. But planning, properly done, always allows better use of time. Plan your work with at least as much care as you plan your vacation.

You may believe that in your particular job planning is useless, since your days are never typical and plans never work out. Realize that even nonroutine jobs involve patterns of behavior. Perhaps you have never recognized the patterns in your work. Get data. Analyze it. Find the patterns. You will then be able to plan your time productively.

Inadequate job descriptions and confusion over responsibilities and authority can make it difficult to set objectives and priorities. Identify the key results you are seeking. Update job descriptions. Make sure all your people know what they're expected to do.

Try separating your activities on the basis of how much they contribute to your objectives. You might use a simple ABC system:

A   They contribute a lot.
B   They contribute somewhat.
C   They contribute little if at all.

Approached in this fashion, priorities almost set themselves.

As noted earlier, many administrators have been successful without planning. They fail to recognize that success sometimes comes in spite of their actions, not because of their actions. These administrators are setting a poor example for their subordinates, who may not be so lucky and who should be learning better habits. If you've been somewhat successful without planning, think how much more successful you might be if you spent more time planning. Planned results are almost always better than chance results.

MEETINGS

Time wasted in meetings must be approached from two points of view: those meetings you call, and those meetings you attend. For both kinds you must consider activities before, during, and after the meeting. This section will focus first on meetings you call, and then show you how the same points can be applied to meetings you attend.

Discourage and discontinue unnecessary meetings. A meeting should not be an excuse for the failure to act independently. No meeting should be called without a definite purpose. Before you call a meeting, determine what you wish to accomplish. Many meetings will be ended right then.

Learn to make decisions without meetings. Never use a committee if you can make the decision yourself. In most hospitals things are "committeed" to death. Administrators are paid to make decisions and to act on them. Think through your own problems before carrying them to others. Don't worry about reaching a consensus. It isn't always necessary to talk an idea over and make sure everybody buys it. Instead, make the decision, delegate it, and then ask for compliance from competent administrators.

Don't call meetings simply because you don't want to address an issue. Often, the best way to avoid a decision is to initiate a "study of the problem." Make-work studies must be separated from the legitimate studies needed to establish a sense of direction or to implement a plan. In-house studies are one of the prime activity traps of administrators.

Whenever you must hold a meeting, develop an agenda and stick to it. Prepare the agenda ahead of time. If this isn't possible, take the first few minutes of the meeting to set the agenda for participants. Resist interruptions and stay on course. Insist that others be prepared for the meeting.

Set a time limit for all meetings. Start on time and end on time. You will probably find that you can accomplish just as much in far less time than you have in the past. Don't wait for slow people to show up before starting. If you hold up a meeting for stragglers, you only guarantee that people will continue to be slow showing up in the future.

Invite only those whose attendance is necessary and tell them exactly what will be expected of them. Allow people to come and go as their contribution is needed. There is no point having people sit all the way through a meeting if only a few minutes of it are significant to them.

Analyze each of your meetings from time to time. Are the right people attending? Are too many people attending? Are people properly prepared? Is the meeting held at the proper time, in the proper place? How could your meetings be improved?

Don't make people more comfortable during a meeting than necessary. In other words, don't give people two-hour chairs if you intend to keep them for only 30 minutes. You might even try holding some stand-up meetings.

Be sure that follow-up is prompt. Summarize conclusions. Make sure people know exactly what they are supposed to do and when they should do it. If minutes are required, make sure they are distributed within 48 hours of the meeting. Instead of assigning this task to a meeting participant, bring in a secretary for the sole purpose of recording, typing, and distributing the minutes.

As a meeting participant, you can encourage these same time-saving procedures. Be prepared yourself. Come on time. Don't contribute to irrelevant or unnecessary talk. Encourage others to stick to the point. Ask the meeting leader to establish an agenda and a follow-up system. Be the kind of participant you would like to have when you're chairing the meeting.

Many administrators complain that they have no influence over improving meetings, but this is simply not true. If all participants requested improvements in meetings, very few meeting leaders would be able to resist the requests. It is precisely because participants accept ineffective meetings that ineffective meetings continue.

PAPERWORK—MEMOS, MAIL, REPORTS, READING

No administrator likes paperwork. But administrators seem to be engaging in more paperwork every year. Paperwork will probably continue to consume an even greater amount of your time unless you take strong action to contain it.

In a recent ad, the Xerox Corporation pointed out that the one American resource that is mushrooming rather than dwindling is information. "With 72 billion new pieces of information arriving yearly," the ad asks, "how do you cope with it all?" That's not an idle question. There are several things you can do to prevent the paperwork dragon from swallowing you, your people, and your hospital. Here are five important guidelines:

1. Don't record it.
2. Don't ask for it.
3. Throw it away.
4. Discontinue it.
5. Question its purpose and continued existence.

Get off mailing lists when the information no longer contributes to your objectives. Cancel unnecessary subscriptions. Do everything you can to cut the flow to your in-basket. Write less. Use the telephone more.

Periodically recheck the value of every report to make sure it is still needed. Be sure that everyone receiving a copy truly needs a copy. Are you sure you couldn't eliminate one or two? Perhaps you could combine two or more reports. Try discontinuing a questionable report temporarily just to see how much it is missed. Make a check periodically to find out how many reports are being thrown away or distributed without your knowledge.

Examine report cycles to see if they could be lengthened. For example, instead of a weekly report, perhaps a monthly report would do. Make sure that all reports are issued on time. Stress the importance of brevity and simplicity in all written material. If reports are longer than a few pages, include a summary of the highlights at the beginning to save time for those recipients who aren't concerned with the details.

Weigh the cost of spending time collecting and compiling information against the benefits of having it available. Don't overdo revisions in the name of perfection when the added benefits are small or nonexistent. Consider the possibility of substituting oral reports for written reports. Look for new ways to use recording equipment in an effort to save paperwork. Most administrators would rather talk than write, so this approach has definite possibilities.

Write for the receiver, using a clear, concise, fact-oriented style. Use short, simple, everyday language. Eliminate unnecessary words, sentences, and paragraphs. There's nothing wrong with one-paragraph letters. Answer correspondence by making handwritten responses in the margins of the letters you receive and mailing them back to the senders.

Be selective in what you read. Learn to read faster and better. Scan, look for major ideas and important details, and seek out the logic of the article.

Sort through all the items that cross your desk. Try to handle each piece of paper only once. Don't set aside a piece of paper requiring action without taking some action. If you do shunt it aside, it will come back to haunt you later.

Think before you write or dictate. Plan what you want to say. Use the best dictating equipment you can find. Investigate the various uses of word processing systems and computerized information systems.

LEAVING TASKS UNFINISHED; JUMPING FROM ONE TASK TO ANOTHER

Jumping from task to task results when an administrator is personally disorganized, has no sense of priorities, or tries to do everything. Often "task jumping" is simply a bad habit. The suggestions outlined in Chapters 3 and 6 can be of assistance here. Clarifying objectives and planning your time will help you reduce your tendency to jump from task to task.

Learn to focus on one activity at a time. Follow each activity through to conclusion before picking up another. Unless an emergency arises, resist other people's attempts to engage you in a task before you have finished the task you are working on.

Develop a sense of priorities by focusing on the most important items first. Arrange your day so that you work on important items in the morning. Do the things you dislike earlier in the day.

ATTEMPTING TOO MUCH AT ONCE

Administrators often attempt to do too much at once because they are unable to say no. Like it or not, you must say no. This little two-letter word is probably the greatest time-saving expression in the English language.

Recognize that no matter how well organized you are, you simply cannot do everything. In order to get good results consistently, you must focus on important tasks. This means that you will have to set aside many unimportant tasks. Don't worry about offending people. As people learn that you really do focus on important items first, and get results, they will probably follow your example. Trying to help everyone on every request is the best way to help the fewest people with the poorest results.

If you can't say no because you lack assertiveness, take a class on assertiveness training or read a good book on the subject. Learn to recognize that you have rights just as other people do. Saying yes to everyone is not necessarily the best way to gain people's respect. Quite often, it's the best way to allow people to take advantage of you.

When you must say no, give people an alternative. Perhaps you can do it at another time, or perhaps you know someone else who can help. State your reason for saying no. Explain that there are other things that simply have higher priority. Do not blame somebody else for your refusal in an effort to create the impression that it isn't really your fault. Be decisive. Take responsibility for your own actions. Don't postpone the chore. When you are forced to say no, do it as quickly as possible.

Another major reason administrators attempt too much at once is that they do not accurately estimate the amount of time an activity will take. The planning approach described in Chapter 6 will help you learn to make better time estimates. Break down each task into a series of steps. Estimate the minimum amount of time required for each step. Add up all the estimates to determine the total amount of time necessary for that task. Recognize that this is the bare minimum, and that the actual time will probably be much higher.

When all your time is committed, don't take on another commitment unless you drop an earlier one. If superiors attempt to force additional commitments on you, ask which project should be dropped in order to take on the new project. Don't force projects on subordinates without considering that they might be in the same dilemma.

Learn to be realistic about how much you can actually accomplish. This doesn't mean that you should cut back on your activities to the point where you're doing very little. It does mean that you should recognize your limitations and work within them. Do as much as you can, stretch a little, but don't take on more than you can get done.

You can work on only one thing at a time. And you can balance only so many tasks at once. When you try to exceed this limit, your performance in many activities will suffer.

INDECISION AND PROCRASTINATION

– The big reason for indecision is the fear of being wrong, or the strong desire to be right. You delay making decisions until you have all possible information, or you put off the decision in the hope that you won't have to decide or that someone else will take the responsibility off your shoulders.

Realize that you will never be able to get all the information you would like to have before deciding. Make decisions even when some facts are missing. Some risk is inevitable. You may also need to improve your fact-finding procedures. Could you get more information another way? Could you get information quicker? Could you get more accurate information? Analyze your decision-making methods and look for ways to improve.

Part of the fear of deciding comes from having made mistakes in the past. Mistakes are frequently caused by failing to realize that every act creates both desirable and undesirable consequences. Anticipating both the positive and negative effects helps minimize your risk.

Many administrators waste a lot of time rehashing former decisions, explaining bad ones, or trying to salvage things that should have been written off and forgotten. Don't waste time regretting failures. Learn from the past and use it as a guide for the future, not as an excuse for failing to deal with the present.

There's a time for deliberating and a time for deciding. Learn when it's time to stop investigating and make the decision. Don't go overboard gathering additional bits and pieces of information that will add little if anything to the quality of your decision. Make the decision and get on with it. And don't agonize about the decision for days afterward.

– Procrastination usually results from a desire to avoid unpleasant things. Often the best way to handle unpleasant tasks is to do them first. Schedule your most distasteful chore at the beginning of the day and get it behind you, rather than dreading it and continually putting it off. You should also consider the cost of delay. If the task must eventually be done, the work involved may expand with procrastination. If you wait until the last minute, you will have to work under increased pressure.

The longer you wait, the greater the number of things that can go wrong.

Try analyzing each unpleasant task. What exactly makes it unpleasant? Learn to confront the unpleasantness and deal with it directly. Many people challenge themselves to do at least one thing they dread every month, simply because they don't want to do it.

Sometimes it helps to tackle an unpleasant task by dividing it into small pieces that can be done for five or ten minutes at a time. Once you get moving, you may find that the task is not so unpleasant after all. And even if you do quit in a few minutes, you'll still gain on the task. For example, many administrators delay writing reports. One way to get started is to begin making notes on the points you need to cover. You can approach the report one section at a time or even one page at a time. There are any number of ways you can tackle an unpleasant task in small bits and pieces.

Set a deadline for the task. The pressure of a deadline, even a self-imposed one, can be sufficient to move you to action. Make sure your deadline is realistic, and put it in writing. Post the deadline on the wall, set it on your desk, or put it wherever you will see it frequently. Tell other people about your deadline. You may break commitments you make to yourself, but you are not so likely to break those you make to others.

Promise yourself a reward for completing the task. The reward can be anything that appeals to you, large or small. There are two main points to remember here: If you don't earn the reward, don't give it to yourself; and if you do earn it, be sure to take it. Occasional rewards can make life more enjoyable and help you conquer your procrastination.

The desire for perfection is another cause of procrastination. Authors who keep rewriting the first chapter, striving for the perfect phrase, seldom publish books. Administrators who keep pushing their subordinates for perfect results seldom achieve them. Perfectionism leads to greater anxiety and tension and strained relationships between people. It accomplishes little. Learn to do your best the first time around, and call it good.

Procrastination can also be traced to vague fears that something will go wrong. Instead of putting things off and worrying, focus on what you wish to accomplish. Write out all the possible obstacles that could prevent you from achieving your goal. Then look over each obstacle and think of various ways you might overcome it. Write down all the possible solutions and pick the ones most likely to work. You now have the basis for a positive plan of action.

Another technique for overcoming vague fears is to develop a worry list. Write down all the things you think might go wrong. Keep the list. From time to time read it over and note what has actually happened in each instance. You will probably find that many of the things you worry about never happen. A worry list can help you learn to worry less.

Perhaps the most valuable thing you can do when you are procrastinating is to admit it. Once you acknowledge that you are indeed procrastinating, examine your situation and try to determine why. Then find some technique for conquering your procrastination. Procrastination can become a habit. Procrastination breeds procrastination. Analyzing your habits and making a list of all the things you tend to put off may help you find the pattern to your procrastination. Use this knowledge to change your do-it-later tendency into a do-it-now habit.

CLUTTERED DESK OR OFFICE

The cluttered desk syndrome generally results from sloppy work habits. People with disorganized desks fall victim to Douglass's Law: "Clutter tends to expand to fill the space available for its retention."

Most of the clutter on your desk is probably paper. Your objective in handling paper is to keep it moving. Don't let it settle on your desk. Try to handle each piece of paper only once. Don't lay it aside to be dealt with later; do it now. Throw it away, file it, or initiate action on it—but don't just bury it in a pending file.

Don't record things you don't really need. Get off mailing lists. Stop asking for things. Learn to use your wastebasket more often. Realize that you can work on only one project at a time.

That project should be the only thing on your desk. If other things are there, you are more likely to be distracted. Put everything else in a proper place until you need it.

Set up a filing system that allows you to retrieve information easily. Develop a system for screening mail so your secretary can stop some of the paper flow. Keep track of your paper for a month and look for patterns. What's really important? What have you really used? Which paper contributes and which paper doesn't?

View your desk as a work tool. Think about its proper function—helping you be more effective. It should not serve as a storage center for all that junk. Throw away the junk. Don't clear your desk by putting the junk in the drawers. Put it in the wastebasket instead.

Develop a set of criteria for determining what stays on top of your desk. Get into the habit of thinking that there is a place for everything, and learn to put everything in its place. Reduce the clutter and you reduce the distractions that divert your attention from the task at hand.

Develop the art of wastebasketry. Learn to throw things out. Get a second wastebasket. Get a larger wastebasket. Throw away everything you possibly can. You can probably throw out 20 percent of the paper in your office and never miss it.

FAILURE TO DO FIRST THINGS FIRST

Failure to do first things first frequently results from the failure to identify what "first things" are. This happens when people do not take enough time to think, analyze, and plan.

Every administrator's job should include some time each day for just thinking. Start by setting aside 15 minutes a day for thinking. As you get used to it, gradually increase the amount of time.

Ask yourself how things could be done better. Think about ways to improve your job performance. Establish a quiet hour in your office, some time each day to think and plan.

Don't make unnecessary assumptions. Check things out; get

clarification. Identify your behavior patterns and work on developing better habits. Start your day by working on the most important item first. Then go to the second most important item.

TRAVEL, WAITING, COMMUTING

Time spent traveling or waiting is often considered dead time by administrators. Certainly, there are only a limited number of things you can do while you are traveling or waiting. However, there are many ways to turn this otherwise "dead" time into useful, productive time.

The first step is to analyze your work to determine which tasks you can do most easily when traveling or waiting. Set the tasks aside for those occasions. For example, try dictating reports, action notes, memos, or letters in your car or in a plane. Listen to tapes as you drive. Have someone else do the driving so you will have more leeway in using travel time productively. Instead of driving to the office, consider buses, trains, or carpools.

Save secondary reading material for trips and waiting time. Follow good time management principles on trips as well as in the office. Dictate all reports and correspondence generated during your trip before you return home. Consider the paperwork an integral part of the trip. Do it as you go along. Use the newer, small dictating machines that block out background noises. You will be able to dictate on jet planes and still be heard clearly.

ROUTINE AND TRIVIA

It is easy to rid yourself of routine, trivial tasks if you learn to emphasize results instead of activities. Think about your objectives. How do routine, trivial tasks add to your effectiveness?

Work smarter, not harder. It's not how much you do that counts, but how much you get done. Don't do your own typing, filing, or other clerical work. Use dictating equipment instead of writing letters by hand. If you rid yourself of trivial tasks, you will have more time to devote to the important things that are not getting done.

Review routine tasks. What would happen if they weren't done at all? If the answer is nothing, stop doing them. Eliminate all unnecessary activities. Delegate all nonessential or non-critical activities as far down as possible.

Do important things first; do routine things last. Don't fill prime morning hours with trivial activities. And don't waste your peak performance periods on anything less than highly important activities. Practice being efficient in performing routine tasks. Analyze them and look for shortcuts. Could they be done by machine? Could tasks be combined or modified? Don't get involved in "busywork" to fill gaps in your time. And don't justify spending time on routine things by telling yourself you are getting them out of the way so you'll be free to tackle bigger things later. Later may never come.

Eliminating time wasters will undoubtedly require a change in habits on your part. Since habits are resistant to change, don't expect miracles. Review the process for changing habits described in Chapter 2. Begin to build your new time habits in the same way you developed your bad time habits—by repeating the behavior until it becomes automatic. This will require considerable effort and discipline in the beginning. Don't try to change all your time habits at once. If you do, you are almost certain to fail. Work on developing new techniques for eliminating your biggest time waster first. Then go on to your next biggest time waster. Approaching time wasters methodically, one at a time, will help ensure their elimination.

Resolve to eliminate one time waster each week. This resolution will force you to continually examine how you use your time. Identifying time wasters is the first step to eliminating them. If you can eliminate one time waster from your life each week, you will undoubtedly become one of the truly effective administrators. You and your hospital will both benefit.

8
WORKING
WITH
OTHERS

Of all the best leaders, when their task is accomplished, their work done, the people remark, 'We have done it ourselves.'

LAO-TZU

Running a modern hospital is not a do-it-yourself job. No one lives in a vacuum. Many people must cooperate if things are to happen right. Working with others on your staff, however, can be both rewarding and frustrating.

Many books have been written on staff development. In this chapter, we will focus on three primary concerns: (1) balancing conflicts in time priorities, (2) extending time management concepts to others around you, and (3) learning to delegate effectively.

CONFLICTS IN PRIORITIES

Conflicts are a way of life in any organization. The conflicts are not necessarily intentional; they often arise because of differences in how people perceive events. Superiors and subordinates frequently have differing views of what is most important and what ought to be done first. Unfortunately, there seems to be very little dialogue between superiors and subordinates concerning these differences. Little honest effort is made to resolve conflicts in a way that will enable both superiors and subordinates to function more effectively.

Conflicts often occur because of activity traps. Administrators tend to become so engrossed in their activities that they lose sight of the purpose behind the activities. They fall into activity traps by focusing on activities when they should be focusing on objectives. The result is that they and their subordinates often see objectives and priorities differently.

In his book *Management and the Activity Trap* (New York: Harper & Row, 1974), George Odiorne suggests a technique to help clarify and resolve these perceptual conflicts. To begin with, the superior should write a list of the major responsibilities of the subordinate. For each area of responsibility, the superior should define the intended result. The subordinate should then write a similar list independent of the superior. The subordinate should examine his or her job in terms of the following questions: "What are my major areas of responsibility? In each area of responsibility, what results do I think the boss expects?"

When the lists are completed, they should be compared. According to Odiorne, the results will often look like this: On recurring, ongoing responsibilities, the average superior and subordinate, caught in activity traps, will fail to agree on at least 15 percent of the items. As a result of this failure to agree on regular responsibilities, superior and subordinate will disagree at least 50 percent of the time on what major problems exist and should be solved. Worst of all, superior and subordinate will probably fail to agree 90 percent of the time on what needs changing or improvement.

Discovering the nature of disagreements between superior and subordinate will not automatically solve the problem. However, with this kind of information the next step can be defined more clearly. Superior and subordinate must develop a working consensus on important issues, important results, and priorities for working on them.

Ultimately, the only way to resolve differences in priority perceptions is to develop an ongoing dialogue with your subordinates. You must regularly discuss objectives, intended results, priorities, and appropriate methods with your staff. These conversations must involve a great deal of give-and-take. They should not be one-way communication.

Effective administrators discover many ways to develop a continuing conversation with their staff about how to use time best. They find ways to talk about time waste without blaming others. They realize that it does no good to complain to outsiders about how badly time is wasted by people in their organization. They know that they must talk to the people who are both part of the problem and part of the solution.

THE GROUP TIME WASTER PROFILE

One good way to develop a time management dialogue with your staff is to construct a group time waster profile. Below is a list of the most frequently mentioned time wasters:

1. Interruptions—drop-in visitors, distractions, telephone calls.
2. Becoming involved in too much detail or too many routine tasks.
3. Crises, emergencies, firefighting.
4. Lack of objectives or deadlines; personal disorganization.
5. Meetings—scheduled or unscheduled.
6. Paperwork—memos, mail, reports, reading.
7. Leaving tasks unfinished; jumping from one task to another.
8. Attempting too much at once.
9. Procrastination, indecision, daydreaming.
10. Ineffective communication and feedback.
11. Lack of self-discipline.

12. Cluttered desk or office; general disorder.
13. Ineffective delegation.
14. Inability to say no.
15. Socializing or idle conversation.
16. Constantly switching priorities.
17. Failure to do first things first.
18. Travel, waiting, commuting.

Give a copy of this list to everyone on your staff. Ask each person to identify his or her top six time wasters. If some people's time wasters are not on the list, have them add their time wasters at the bottom. Each person's top six time wasters should be weighted as follows: The No. 1 time waster should be assigned a weight of 30; the No. 2 time waster, a weight of 25; the No. 3 time waster, a weight of 20; and so on down to the No. 6 time waster, which should be given a weight of 5.

When everyone has ranked and weighted his or her top six time wasters, combine the lists. Many people will have identified the same time wasters; some people will have time wasters that others do not have. Add the weights together and prepare a final list of time wasters and weights. The time waster with the heaviest overall weighting becomes the No. 1 group time waster. If you were to focus on improving the time waster, the greatest benefit would accrue to the greatest number of people.

If the subject of time waste is approached in a nonthreatening manner, without pinning the blame on anyone, people will generally discuss how they use their time openly. The discussion will quickly produce ideas about how wasted time might be eliminated or reduced. At this point, you have the beginning of a group action plan.

The group time waster profile is also a valuable tool for discussing good time use with your staff. In other words, if the group actually were able to recover some wasted time, how should it be spent? Why should time be spent on those particular activities? The discussion should move toward intended results and planning. When you focus on discussing objectives and plans for accomplishing those objectives, you will discover ways in which everyone can use time more effectively.

A principle to be considered in managing group time is this: Don't expect subordinates to manage their time well if you're not managing your time well—people tend to follow your example. In other words, don't try to extend time management concepts to your staff until you have learned how to use them yourself. Clean up your own job first.

Administrators frequently discover a good time management concept and immediately think of at least one subordinate who could benefit from it. For example, you've just been thinking about time logs and it occurs to you that "George could really use a time log to get hold of his job!" If you have never done a time log yourself, don't expect George to favor the idea when you discuss it with him. Do a time log of your own job. Discover your own problems and work out ways to solve them. Then go to George and tell him what you have done, how the time log was beneficial to you, and what you have learned from doing it. With this approach, George is far more likely to undertake a time log of his own.

MANAGING GROUP TIME

Extending time concepts to your staff is part of regular training and development. To develop your staff, you must be committed. You must utilize good time management concepts. You must have your own time in control. You must be patient. You must know more than your subordinates. You must have good judgment about your subordinate's developmental needs.

In short, developing staff requires a tremendous amount of your time. Unfortunately, many administrators let staff development slide to the end of the line. Then they try to improve staff performance by exhorting people to utilize good time management principles. If you do one thing and say another, subordinates will follow the example of your actions.

To gain a quick focus on time problems and how you, as a superior, can be most beneficial, ask your staff the following questions:

1. What do I do that wastes your time and hinders your performance?
2. What could I do to help you make better use of your time and achieve greater results?

Every administrator should regularly pose these two questions to each staff member. If you have never asked your staff such questions, don't expect an instant response. At first, your subordinates may seem a bit suspicious. They will probably think, "I wonder what the boss is up to now." Don't worry. Just keep asking the questions. If you are sincere in your efforts and are willing to listen and to act on people's responses, you will soon find a better dialogue developing between you and your staff. This dialogue should ultimately center on intended results.

Before focusing on results from your staff, focus on yourself. Ask your staff members: "How could I manage my time better?" Many of your people will undoubtedly see your time wasters more clearly than you do. It is always easier to see another person's problems. Be willing to listen to justified criticism from your staff.

The success of your time management dialogue will ultimately depend on the communications climate in your hospital. You and your staff must be able to talk honestly with one another. In a positive, open atmosphere this is not difficult. In a negative, hostile atmosphere, it may be impossible. However, if this kind of conversation does not take place, much time will undoubtedly be lost. The result will be poor communications habits, time wasted in activity traps, scapegoating, dysfunctional hospital politics, staff members trying to outmaneuver one another, and other equally destructive behaviors.

Many hospital administrators are anxious to extend good time management principles to their staff. There is good reason for doing so. If everyone in your hospital were using his or her time in the best way possible, total productivity would jump. You'd be able to accomplish far more than you do at present. This desire for improving staff time use has led many hospital administrators to attend time management seminars. A seminar provides a welcome opportunity to break away from the hectic pace long enough to think about what is happening. At these seminars administrators often gain a new insight into their time problems and a commitment to seeking improvement.

But what happens? They attempt to translate their motivation and commitment into action by presenting their new ideas to superiors, peers, and subordinates. They are met with responses varying from "So what?" to "That sounds like a good idea—maybe we'll look into it sometime." The people back home may agree intellectually, but they haven't gained the same insight that the administrator has in attending the seminar.

Many administrators have solved this problem by exposing other people in their hospital to time management workshops. At these workshops, everyone hears the same material. Everyone has time to understand and absorb the concepts. Everyone has an opportunity to think about and discuss the main issues. People begin to develop a sense of togetherness, with the focus on how to make better use of their time.

If these workshops are done well, people will typically emerge with a list of several things to implement immediately—things that will make a significant difference in your operation. Further, they will be committed to these actions and to supporting each other's improvement efforts. Morale will improve as people feel more in tune with the total operation. And there will usually be an increase in productivity of at least 10 percent.

What do you think would happen if your staff attended a time management workshop? Do you think the benefits would be worth the probable costs of such a workshop? Weigh the pros and cons by completing the checklist shown on page 105.

DELEGATING TO OTHERS

Delegation is perhaps the greatest tool available to administrators for developing capable subordinates, improving results, and gaining more time. How well do you delegate? Answer the questions on page 106 as honestly as you can.

Possible Results of Having Staff Attend a Time Management Workshop

	PROBABILITY OF THIS HAPPENING				
POSITIVE	**HIGH**				**LOW**
1. Staff would favor the idea.	☐	☐	☐	☐	☐
2. It would raise everyone's awareness about the importance of using time more effectively.	☐	☐	☐	☐	☐
3. A "quiet hour" could be instituted for everyone.	☐	☐	☐	☐	☐
4. Coordination and cooperation would increase.	☐	☐	☐	☐	☐
5. Time spent in meetings would be reduced.	☐	☐	☐	☐	☐
6. Staff could initiate priority-setting conferences.	☐	☐	☐	☐	☐
7. Interruptions would be reduced for everyone.	☐	☐	☐	☐	☐
8. People would start planning better.	☐	☐	☐	☐	☐
9. Morale would be improved.	☐	☐	☐	☐	☐
10. Staff could get rid of unproductive activities.	☐	☐	☐	☐	☐
11. Other offices would be impressed.	☐	☐	☐	☐	☐
12. Productivity would increase by at least 10 percent.	☐	☐	☐	☐	☐
13. If successful, workshop would help me personally.	☐	☐	☐	☐	☐
14. Other:	☐	☐	☐	☐	☐
15. Other:	☐	☐	☐	☐	☐
NEGATIVE					
1. Upper management might be hard to convince.	☐	☐	☐	☐	☐
2. Some people might find it threatening.	☐	☐	☐	☐	☐
3. If not successful, I would be blamed.	☐	☐	☐	☐	☐
4. Other:	☐	☐	☐	☐	☐
5. Other:	☐	☐	☐	☐	☐

How Well Do You Delegate?

	YES	NO
1. Do you allow your people to make mistakes?		
2. Do your people make most of the day-to-day decisions without your approval?		
3. Do your people get promotions at least as frequently as other people with equivalent responsibility in your hospital?		
4. Do you frequently take work home or work late at the office?		
5. Does your operation function smoothly when you're absent?		
6. Do you spend more time working on details than you do on planning and supervision?		
7. Do your people feel they have sufficient authority over personnel, finances, facilities, and other resources?		
8. Do your people think that more tasks should be delegated to them?		
9. Is your follow-up procedure adequate?		
10. Do you overrule or reverse decisions made by your subordinates?		
11. Do you bypass your subordinates by making decisions that are part of their jobs?		
12. Do you do things that your subordinates could and should be doing?		
13. If you were incapacitated for six months, is there someone who could readily take your place?		
14. Do your key people delegate well to their own subordinates?		
15. Will there be a big pile of paper requiring your action when you return from a trip or absence?		
16. Do your subordinates take the initiative in expanding their authority with delegated projects without waiting for you to initiate assignments?		

If you are an effective delegator, you answered yes to questions 1, 2, 3, 5, 7, 9, 13, 14, and 16 and no to the other questions. Did you get all 16 correct? If you did, good for you! You can probably skip the rest of this chapter. If, on the other hand, you missed several questions, this chapter may be very valuable in helping you learn to be a better delegator.

Delegation can be defined as appointing someone else to act on your behalf. It means asking a subordinate to do something that is normally part of your responsibility.

Many administrators are confused about the difference between delegation and job assignment. Consider the following statement: "Delegation should always include the results to be achieved as well as the activities to be performed." Do you agree or disagree? If you agree with the statement, you are probably assigning jobs when you think you are delegating. Work assignment is simply instructing a subordinate to complete a particular task in a specific manner.

In delegating, you must give the subordinate four things:

1. Responsibility and accountability for completing the assignment.
2. Sufficient authority to complete the assignment.
3. Sufficient power to make the decisions needed to complete the assignment.
4. Sufficient freedom of action to complete the assignment properly.

If any of these four elements is missing, your delegation efforts will probably be unsuccessful. Frustration and disillusionment will result for both you and your subordinate.

Some administrators believe that when they delegate, they gain time and also relieve themselves of responsibility. This is not true. You never delegate responsibility. Those things for which you were responsible before delegation you are still responsible for after delegation. What you delegate is the authority to act.

The process of delegation actually creates more total responsibility within the hospital. You are responsible to your superiors for some set of results. When you delegate to a subordinate,

you are still responsible for those results. However, not only are
you responsible to your superior, but now your subordinate is
responsible to you for some portion of the overall results. Total
responsibility has increased.

Delegating the authority to act is not a black-or-white issue.
Authority is delegated in varying degrees. There are six general
levels of delegated authority:

Level 6   Take action—no further contact with me required.
Level 5   Take action—let me know what you did.
Level 4   Look into it—let me know what you intend to do;
            do it unless I say no.
Level 3   Look into it—let me know what you intend to do;
            don't take action until I approve.
Level 2   Look into it—let me know possible actions; state
            pros and cons of each and recommend one for my
            approval.
Level 1   Look into it—report all the facts to me; I'll decide
            what to do.

The degree of authority you grant to a subordinate will depend on many things, including the complexity or importance
of the project, the subordinate's expertise, the time constraints
on the project, and your confidence and trust in the subordinate. As you train and develop subordinates, you will move
from lower levels of authority to higher levels. You should not
delegate the same level of authority to an untrained subordinate
that you would to a trained subordinate.

However, many administrators delegate by rote, without
thinking about appropriate authority levels. To discover your
own delegation pattern, fill out the responsibility–authority
chart in Figure 13. Do a chart for each of your subordinates.
List all delegated assignments, along with the level of authority
granted to the subordinate. Look for patterns. Do you tend to
delegate at the same levels for all subordinates? Do you always
delegate at low levels for some subordinates but at high levels
for other subordinates? Why or why not? Have you consciously
considered the appropriate level of authority for each delegated

Figure 13. Responsibility–authority chart.

SUBORDINATE'S NAME_____

PROJECTS OR RESPONSIBILITIES	LEVEL OF AUTHORITY					
	1	2	3	4	5	6

assignment? Analyzing the charts will undoubtedly help you spot areas where you can improve your delegation efforts.

Administrators tend to be like their administrators, who tend to be like their administrators, who tend to be like their administrators, and so on. If delegation is ineffective at the top, delegation will probably be ineffective at the bottom. Therefore, improvement must begin at the top.

IMPROVING YOUR DELEGATION SKILLS

To improve your delegation skills, consider the following guidelines:

1. *Analyze your job*
   What are your objectives?
   What results are expected of you?
   What do you do?
   Can anyone else do it for you now?
   Can anyone be trained to do it?
   Do your superiors agree with your job analysis?
2. *Decide what to delegate*
   Review the decisions you make most often.

Consider the functions that make you "overspecialized."

Assess the areas in which your staff is better qualified.

Assess the areas you dislike (but remember to delegate both the good and the bad).

Review the areas in which subordinates need development.

Think of things that will add variety to a subordinate's job.

3. *Plan the delegation*

Strive for "whole job" unity.

Review all essential details and decisions.

Clarify appropriate limits of authority.

Establish performance standards.

Determine feedback controls, including what information is needed, how often, and in what form.

Provide for training, coaching, or backup people.

Follow this guideline: If you can't control it, don't delegate it.

4. *Select the right person*

Consider the subordinate's interests and abilities.

Assess the degree of challenge.

Determine who needs it most.

Try to balance and rotate items.

5. *Delegate effectively.*

Clarify the results intended and the priorities involved.

Clarify the degree of authority and other operating parameters.

Stress the importance of the job.

Take time to communicate effectively.

6. *Follow up*

Insist on timely information.

Act promptly.

Insist on results, but not on perfection.

Encourage independence.

Learn to live with differences.

Don't short-circuit assignments.

Reward good performance.

Realize that effective delegation requires a minimal level of trust between you and your subordinates. Trust takes time to develop. Delegation works best when there is a favorable organizational climate, with an emphasis on employee development, growth, innovation, creativity, and human dignity. If your hospital does not foster such a climate, the organizational atmosphere will have to be improved before delegation can be truly effective.

Remember, too, that delegation should flow downward but not upward. Upward delegation is a fact of life in almost any organization. It begins innocently enough, and the result is always the same. The superior winds up making decisions and doing work that the subordinate should be attending to.

It happens quite easily. You're walking down the hallway of the hospital one day when you pass one of your subordinates, who says, "Hi, boss. By the way, we have a problem with XYZ." You must be very careful of that "we." "We" may mean that the subordinate has a problem he or she wants to shift to you. Still, being a concerned superior and wanting to help, you probably say something like this: "You're right, that's quite a problem. I'll have to check into it and get back to you."

The moment a subordinate hits you with a problem, you face an impossible dilemma. You know just enough to get involved but not enough to solve the problem right there on the spot. This means that the ball is now in your court. The next step is up to you, not the subordinate. In fact, several days later the subordinate may pop into your office and say, "Boss, about that problem we were discussing the other day. How are you coming?" This is called supervision.

Your challenge at all times is to make sure that the people who work on problems are the ones who should be working on the problems. This means that when subordinates bring you problems you must help them become good problem solvers. You cannot do this by solving subordinates' problems for them; you must teach them how to solve their problems for themselves. If you are the victim of upward delegation, take steps to send the problems back to the people who own them. And resolve in the future never to take on a problem that is not your own.

WORKING WITH YOUR SECRETARY

Probably the most important subordinate for any administrator is the secretary. Secretaries and administrators form a unique team. In a sense, their jobs are a single unit rather than two separate positions. The only rationale for having a secretary in the first place is to enable you to accomplish more than you could accomplish without a secretary. Thinking of yourself and your secretary as a team will enable you to focus on how both of you can use your time more effectively, whether alone or together.

Your secretary is an important member of your staff. Include him or her in staff meetings when appropriate. Be sure that your secretary is given the same training and development opportunities that other members of your staff receive.

Discuss your objectives, priorities, and plans with your secretary every day. Your secretary cannot help you accomplish your objectives if he or she does not know what your objectives are. Outline your plans first thing in the morning. This will help you avoid many of the interruptions that would otherwise fill your day. It will also help you identify potential problems and gain your secretary's assistance in resolving them.

Treat your secretary with dignity and respect. Provide support and backup when necessary. Don't downgrade the secretarial job to a "go-for" position. Keep your secretary fully informed about what is happening. When you leave, be sure your secretary knows where you're going, how you can be reached, and when you will return. Share your ideas about upcoming objectives and projects. If you inform your secretary fully about your affairs, it will be much easier to encourage other people to deal directly with your secretary for many of the things he or she can handle.

Allow your secretary to organize your office procedures. You might even consider having your secretary handle your personal schedule. Find out how and when your secretary would like to schedule activities, such as mail, telephone calls, visitors, meetings, calendars, and filing.

Find out what your secretary would like to know about your projects, objectives, or priorities. Determine what he or she could do that you're now doing. Ask your secretary how you could manage your time better and how he or she could help you manage your time better.

Take time to provide good instruction. Make sure that your secretary understands exactly what you intend. Use good feedback techniques. Allow for initiative and individual differences. Many administrators never seem to have time to provide adequate instructions the first time, but they always have time to do it over. Providing good instructions means being a good listener and encouraging the other person to talk freely.

Remember that a good secretary can double your worth to the hospital, while a poor one can cut it in half. The time and effort you spend developing your secretary will pay many dividends.

GUIDELINES FOR WORKING WITH OTHERS

In working with others to extend time management concepts, you always face the temptation of procrastinating. Staff development is seldom urgent. There always seem to be other things that crowd out developmental effort. Resist the temptation to put off developing your staff. Review the following guidelines often to keep yourself focused on using group time effectively:

1. Don't expect subordinates to manage their time well if you're not managing your time well. They tend to follow your example.

2. Take time to properly train and develop subordinates. It's a key part of your job.

3. Analyze the work flow through your office and look for ways to simplify it.

4. Develop a group time waster profile for your subordinates and discuss how they might eliminate their top time wasters.

5. Make a discussion of better time habits part of the regular performance review. Set improvement objectives.

6. Praise your subordinates' improvement. Don't criticize what remains to be done.

7. Keep subordinates informed about what is happening—changes in objectives, priorities, plans.

8. Use the last few minutes of each staff meeting to discuss ways of spending group time better. Give special emphasis to improving meetings.

9. Discuss your priorities with subordinates and encourage them to discuss their priorities with you. A continuing dialogue is essential if your subordinates are to balance priorities and stay on top of the most important activities.

10. Keep everyone focused on objectives, purposes, and intended results in order to avoid activity traps.

11. Ask your subordinates how you could manage your time better and eliminate some of your time wasters.

12. Ask your subordinates what you do that wastes their time and hinders their effectiveness—and what you could do to help them use their time better.

9
TIME
FOR
YOU

There is more to life than work. One of the prime reasons many administrators become concerned about managing their work time better is so they can reduce their work week and gain more personal time. Time management is important in your personal life just as it is in your work life. The value of work time is usually measured in terms of work-related objectives; the value of personal time is measured in terms of satisfaction and fulfillment.

Many of us are obsessed with time—work time, play time, travel time, leisure time, meal time, next time. Our lives are governed by clocks, calendars, charts, and even phases of the moon. We spend much of our lives as though we were in practice for next time. Seldom do we realize that our lifetimes are determined not just by days and years but by hours and even minutes.

Certainly, not all our time is ours to do with as we please. Our boss, our spouse, our children, our friends, and others all make legitimate demands on our time. Yet we often resist having our time and our lives defined for us.

The paradox of time applies to our personal lives as well as to our work lives. It seems we never have enough time to do everything we'd like to do, yet we have all the time there is. And we always have the time to do what is really important to us. The difficult part is knowing what is important. Many of us actively resist knowing ourselves as well as we must in order to answer that question.

Even when we realize that we can do almost anything we want to, we still find it easier to spend our time according to the way most people spend their time. The question remains: What do we really want to do? If we do not know what we want to do, or who we are, or who we want to be, we are lost. As our lives pass us by, we will come to believe that whatever it was we wanted to do we couldn't do because of the stars, human frailty, or the fear of what others might say. And, finally, we will say there just wasn't enough time.

HOW DO YOU SPEND YOUR TIME?

What do you wish were happening in your life? What do you wish you had time for? The concepts outlined in this book for solving work time problems can also be applied to personal time problems. There are personal activity traps just as there are activity traps in the hospital. You become so engrossed in doing things in your personal life that you stop asking about purpose and value.

The way you spend your time defines the life you live. Thinking about the best way to spend your time means asking about the kind of life you want to lead and the kind of person you want to be.

Most of us operate with a relatively intermediate time horizon. We think in terms of days or weeks and occasionally months. Most of us never think in terms of minutes and, in fact, never consider that idle minutes are a waste of time. Nor do we think in terms of years or lifetimes. We do not realize how all our todays are related to our tomorrows, so we tend to start over each day. As a result, we lead a random sort of existence, with the vague realization that we are going nowhere but without knowing why. We cannot plan for today without also planning for the future. Tomorrow is connected to today just as to-day was connected to yesterday. No one can afford to leave those connections to chance.

Changing the way we use our time requires that we set some goals—goals about what we want to be and do. Uncertainty breeds inactivity. Psychologists have long told us that goals are the keys to successful living. The reason more people are not successful is because they do not select and pursue specific goals. They simply shift from one activity to another without any focus or purpose, naively assuming that things will take care of themselves or will be taken care of by others.

Selecting wise goals is a matter of finding a direction. Life is in the running, not in the arriving. You need to analyze how you spend your time now before you can begin thinking about setting objectives for spending it differently.

YOUR PERSONAL TIME ANALYSIS

Exactly where does your day go? Surveys and ob-servations of several thousand adults indicate that the average day is divided into six major segments, as shown in Figure 14. On the average, people have only about two hours of free time each day—time to do all the things that make life worth living. But by their own account, most people waste at least two hours every day! No wonder so many people feel depressed and dis-satisfied with things in general.

Now, you may raise a question about Saturday and Sunday. Most people work only five days a week. Theoretically, you should have an additional 20 hours on the weekend for en-riching your life. However, hospital administrators usually work more than 40 hours each week. The average administra-tive job consumes 50 to 60 hours weekly. Some administrators regularly work up to 70 hours each week—or more. It comes as no surprise, then, that for many administrators an evening off is a luxury; weekends are lost; time for sleeping and eating gets cut dangerously short; tension and stress build to even higher levels. What better reason for learning to manage your time? It's your life we're talking about!

Figure 14. Where your day goes.

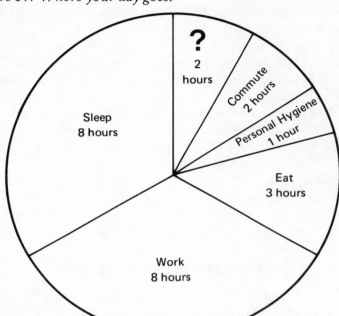

It is important to know how you spend your time. Although you may think you know how you spend your time, you probably don't. Countless studies have shown that most people can't even remember what they did only yesterday or the day before.

The way you spend your time is largely habitual. Thus learning to use your personal time better will probably mean changing some of your personal time habits. But you can't change time habits until you know what those habits are. For the next week or two, try keeping track of your personal time and what you do with it. Be honest with yourself. At the end of each week, summarize your activities. What percentage of time do you spend on each activity? How much of your time is spent on "have to" activities? How much is spent on the things you want to do? Question each activity closely. Is it necessary? What value does it add to your life? What would happen if you didn't do it? Could you spend less time at it and still get acceptable results?

The answers may surprise you. You may discover that the way you spend your personal time is a lot different from what you believed. If so, you are ready to think about changing. Most people usually find this to be one of the most valuable analyses they undertake. It helps them break out of the personal activity traps that prevent them from achieving their goals.

SETTING PERSONAL GOALS

In thinking about personal goals, many administrators immediately focus on career or finances. But there are many other important aspects of life. If you want to feel truly fulfilled and satisfied with yourself, you must determine how to balance these different aspects. You must discover how to do what is really important in each of them. You must consider how you can allocate your time to cover all those areas that are most important to you. Realize that the balance that is appropriate for you may not be appropriate for anyone else. This is a purely personal undertaking.

Setting goals or objectives for different aspects of your life may be a new idea for you. Most of us don't think much about goals. We just respond, or react, to pressures from other people or things. But if you want to control your own time and life, you must decide what your goals are. No one can do this for you. And since you will probably find what you are looking for, it is important that you pursue the right personal goals.

Realize that as your situation changes, your goals may change. As you grow and develop, different things become more or less important. Your goals will change to reflect changes in your values, experiences, and aspirations. But if you do not set goals for yourself, you are likely to find yourself bandied about by all kinds of outside pressures, going first in one direction and then in another. The question remains: What do you want to do with your life?

Many people think of goals in rather vague terms—as happiness, wealth, or fame. But goals mean something more. To have a goal is to have a well-clarified objective, something concrete you wish to attain. If you can determine what you want, you can probably determine how to get it.

Goals should not only be specific and concrete; they should also be attainable. They should make you stretch, but they must be within your reach. Goals should be measurable. Above all, they should be set down in writing, with a time schedule for their achievement. It takes practice to develop a goal that meets all these criteria, but the effort is well worth it. The result is a goal that is truly stimulating, a goal that motivates you to begin pursuing it right away.

Practice your goal-setting skills with the following exercise. Lay out eight sheets of paper. Across the top of each sheet, write down one important aspect of your personal life. For example:

1. Career or vocation.
2. Family and friends.
3. Social, civic, and community relationships.
4. Self-development (mental, educational).
5. Health and physical fitness.
6. Spiritual or religious development.
7. Leisure and recreational activities.
8. Wealth and material possessions.

Once you have labeled the sheets, write down everything you can think of that you would like to accomplish in each area during your lifetime. Don't evaluate anything; just write down your thoughts. Try to fill each sheet of paper. Take as much time as you like. Reach back into your memory for all the things you have ever thought about accomplishing. Write them down. The more ideas you have, the better.

When you have written down everything you can think of, look back and review your lists. Some of the items will be more important to you than others. Since you are after the best use of your time, and since you will not be able to do everything, you need to set priorities. For some people, setting priorities for their personal life is rather frightening. It needn't be. Here is a simple but effective approach.

As you read over the possible objectives on your eight lists, rate them with the ABC method. Put a capital A beside those that are very important to you. Put a B beside those that are moderately important, and put a C beside those that are not too important at all. You now have a simple priority system. If you were to spend your personal time most effectively, you would concentrate on doing the A items first and the B items next, and you would forget about the C items.

Like most people, you probably have several A items on each list. If you do, rank-order them. Go through each list and start with A-1, A-2, A-3, and so forth, until all your A items are ranked. When you have finished, check to see what item is labeled A-1 on each sheet. You might consider putting all the A-1 items on a separate sheet and then ranking them relative to one another. In other words, the various aspects of your life are not equally important. You need to determine which aspects are more important than others. In this way, you can assure yourself of focusing on the most important thing first.

Review your time analysis again. How many of the things you do each day actually relate to your A-1 objectives? Are you spending time in a way that is consistent with achieving your A-1 objectives—or do your activities lead somewhere else? Personal activity traps occur when your daily activities do not lead to your A-1 objectives. Suppose your objective is learning to play the piano. You may have fallen into the activity trap of spending so much time dusting the piano that you never have time to play it. Stop dusting and start playing.

In setting their personal priorities, people often get trapped into thinking that C activities have to be done. This is not always the case. Remember Pareto's Principle, or the 80–20 rule: "80 percent of the value comes from 20 percent of the items, while the remaining 20 percent of the value comes from 80 percent of the items." Apply this rule to your personal objectives. The 20 percent of the items accounting for 80 percent of the value in your life is probably related to your A-1 objectives. The remaining 80 percent of the items accounting for 20 percent of the value in your life probably relates to the C activities you have deluded yourself into doing each day. If you want to become more satisfied with how you use your personal time, learn to concentrate on the high-value activities.

If you don't have time to do your A activities, it's because you are doing all those C activities, not because there isn't enough time.

If you are married, you and your spouse should undertake this lifetime objectives exercise separately. Each of you should list your A-1 objectives—those that are most important to you individually. If you have children, let them participate too. Put all your lists together and examine them carefully. There will probably be some conflicts and some areas that call for negotiation. The members of your family have a legitimate claim on some of your time. Many of your A-1 objectives are likely to relate to family activities. When more than one person is involved, compromise is inevitable. Your challenge is to find a balance that allows all your family members to achieve as many of their A-1 objectives as possible.

PLANNING FOR ACTION

Setting objectives is only the first step in building a more satisfying and fulfilling life. Once you know your objectives, you must build an action plan for accomplishing them. If you want something to happen in your life, you must make a place for it. You must carve out the time and the space which that something demands. Until you do, it won't happen. Things simply won't take care of themselves. If you want to really control your own time, you cannot rely on luck. You must plan.

Plans for accomplishing lifetime objectives may be very long range. Plans for accomplishing objectives for tomorrow are very short range. Over time, however, all those short-range, daily goals should lead to the accomplishment of your long-range goals. So whether it is for tomorrow or for the rest of your life, the system is essentially the same: Identify your objectives, determine your priorities, and decide on your plan of action.

Since lifetime goals may be complex, and since it will probably take some time to accomplish them, it is helpful to break larger goals down into subgoals. Breaking a goal down will make it more believable and more realistic. Smaller goals are more likely to motivate you into taking the first step.

Write down what you will gain by achieving each subgoal. Set a realistic target date for achieving it. Begin to pursue your larger goals by working on these subgoals one at a time. As you achieve each subgoal, you will gain a great deal of confidence and satisfaction. And remember, all the while you will be gaining on your most important lifetime goals.

If you do not have a lot of time each day to devote to your goals, devote as much time as you can. Even 15 minutes a day can make a tremendous difference in your life. In 15 minutes a day, you can learn a foreign language, trace your family history, learn to play a musical instrument, or read a good book.

You can control your time—and your life. In doing so, you will find that you will accomplish more, experience greater satisfaction from the things you are doing, and feel a greater sense of fulfillment. As your feelings of achievement, satisfaction, and fulfillment increase, the quality of your life increases. Your time is your life. As you learn to spend your time better, you create a better life. Satisfaction lies in the accomplishment of the things that are most important to you. This is one of the secrets of success.

Many years ago a man wrote to Ann Landers asking for advice on how to lead a balanced, active, decent life. The writer felt that people tended to get absorbed in work at the expense of human relationships. Ann Landers' response to that letter is worth repeating here:

> The achievers of the world are by nature and training dedicated and highly motivated. Such individuals find it difficult, if not impossible, to lead balanced lives. Success, in this highly complex and competitive world, demands total commitment. The wise movers and shakers realize, however, that there is a point at which they must stop moving and shaking lest they become ingrown, exhausted, victims of total vision, and alas, ineffective. Here is a checklist to keep such people on the beam:
>
> 1. When did you last spend a day or an evening doing something completely frivolous, totally nonproductive? If it's been longer than two months, you are in trouble.

2. Did you spend an evening with friends or attend an affair you have been looking forward to and find that you were too tired to enjoy it? If so, you had better take a close look at your priorities. You are doing too many things and making some bum choices.

3. Have you been telling yourself that you should get a complete physical checkup (including eyes and teeth), but you have been too busy and it will have to wait? If you have been putting it off more than a year, you have not been good to yourself.

4. Do you keep running into people you genuinely enjoy and have been meaning to see, but just haven't gotten around to it? If so, you're cheating yourself. Sit down and schedule time for them, even if it's a dinner or lunch three months away.

5. Can you honestly say you are calm, in control of your life, fulfilled, pleased with yourself, secure in the knowledge that you are making more good decisions than bad ones? If so, you're in very good shape, and you don't need advice from Ann Landers.*

* Copyright 1976 Field Newspaper Syndicate. Reprinted by permission.

10
COMMITMENT
AND
SUCCESS

Why should an administrator become concerned about using time more effectively? Different administrators have different reasons. For some, the prime motivation is the additional money they are likely to obtain with a better job and a more efficient operation. For others, it is the opportunity to expand the programs of their hospital. For some, it means more personal time for fishing or gardening or puttering around the house. For others, it is the increased recognition or prestige they receive when they become known as one of the more effective hospital administrators.

Regardless of what motivates people to improve their time habits, the end result is always the same: Using time better leads to success, regardless of how success is defined. Success is not something that happens by accident. Administrators who have become successful have undoubtedly earned their success. But not everyone who wants to become successful will actually do so.

COMMITMENT AND RESULTS

The primary objective of this book has been to present concepts and techniques that will help hospital administrators improve the use of their time. Perhaps by now you have begun to feel excited about the possibilities; you may even have committed yourself to improvement. It is important, however, that you keep your expectations within bounds. Do not look for instant success. Do not expect to be completely different from the way you were. The habits that govern how you presently use your time were not developed overnight. Changes are not likely to occur overnight either. Only steady, systematic improvement will bring about the results you desire.

Remember, too, that you will never be able to control 100 percent of your time. There are some parts of the day which you simply cannot control. If you can consistently control even 25 percent of your day, you can achieve a significant result. Controlling 25 percent of the day may mean finding no more than one additional hour to use for really important things. Most administrators waste at least an hour each day. Recovering this hour would be well worth the effort.

What might you do with an extra hour each day for the really important things? An hour a day may give you enough time to do the work that you normally carry home each evening. An hour a day may be all the time you need to launch those projects you have not yet implemented. An hour a day may be sufficient time to spend on some of the critical areas of the hospital that need more of your attention. An hour a day may give you an opportunity to develop your staff even better. An hour a day may add another 15 to 30 percent to your personal income. As one administrator put it, "The difference between success and failure is probably no more than one to two hours each day."

MONITORING YOUR PROGRESS

One good way to ensure consistent progress is to monitor your improvement efforts regularly. Your evaluations should focus on the positive. For instance, many administrators would like to become much better at using their time. They may try several approaches, some of which work and some of which do not. In the process, they don't make a huge gain but they do make several small gains. Are they satisfied and encouraged to continue trying? Probably not. People tend to become discouraged when they fail to make huge gains. As long as they continue to focus on what they did not accomplish, instead of on what they did accomplish, they will feel disappointed and are likely to stop trying.

One way to evaluate your progress is to retake the quiz at the end of Chapter 1 periodically to see whether your score improves. If it does, your behavior has probably improved, and you should be producing better results. You might also keep a daily record in diary or journal form of your success in improving how you use your time. Make a note of what you have tried, what seems to work, and what doesn't seem to work. This record can be a valuable source of information for guiding your improvement effort.

You might also consider using graphs or charts to record your progress. Suppose one of your objectives is to reduce the amount of time you spend in meetings. Begin by recording the average amount of time you currently spend in meetings each week. Set a target objective, the amount of time you believe you should spend in meetings. Each week have your secretary keep a record of the time you spend in meetings and post this number on the graph. Your objective, of course, is to have the line on the graph move downward. Each week may not show a decrease over the week before, but if your attempts at improving meetings are successful, the line should generally move downward over a period of weeks.

You can use this same approach to reduce the number of drop-in visitors to your office. Many drop-in visitors are, of course, unnecessary. Determine the average number of drop-in visitors you currently receive each week. Use this figure as the baseline for your graph. If your improvement efforts in the next few weeks are successful, the graph should show a decreasing number of visitors arriving in your office.

If you are truly successful in using your time better, several things should be evident. An analysis of job results should indicate improvement. There should be a significant decrease in the number of recurring crises in your office. Your operations should be running more smoothly. Fewer things should be going wrong. You should be getting more positive feedback in your performance reviews with superiors. There should be fewer things on your list of undone items. You should be able to leave the hospital earlier and spend more time with your family or in personal pursuits. You should feel more on top of the situation, more in control of your job.

Whatever methods you use to evaluate your progress, the important thing is to evaluate it regularly. Any movement in the right direction should be encouraged. You should feel good about the progress you make, no matter how small that progress is. Consistent, small improvements will enable you to make the kinds of long-term gains you desire.

The key to your improvement effort is developing a time management action plan. Clarify your time management objectives, the ways in which you hope to improve the use of your time. Then decide on the actions necessary to accomplish those objectives. Put both the objectives and the actions in writing. Give a copy of your written plan to someone who is important to you. Promise improvement by a certain date. Tackle your improvement effort in progressive steps.

When you begin drafting your action plan, be sure to think about potential obstacles. Obstacles tend to be of two types: those you create yourself and those created by your environment. Both types can prevent you from reaching your time management objectives.

As you uncover potential obstacles, consider how you might overcome them. Some solutions can be implemented immediately. Others will require outside help. Make a note of how other people can help you and ask them in a very positive manner. Do not worry about imposing. Most people are more than willing to help anyone who sincerely wants to improve. Everyone likes to participate in success.

THE SECRET OF SUCCESS

What is the difference between success and failure? Someone once said that the secret of success lies in forming the habit of doing things that failures don't like to do. This, of course, explains why people with obvious qualifications fail, and why people with obvious handicaps manage to overcome them and succeed. It also explains why only a small number of people are successful. Success is not a "natural" state. It is not achieved by following our natural tastes, habits, or preferences.

If the secret of success lies in doing things that failures do not like to do, what are these things? They are the very things that none of us, successes or failures, like to do. Yet successful people do them anyway. For example, successful people take the time to clarify their objectives, even though they know objectives are difficult to clarify. They are willing to plan their time carefully, even though they realize that plans frequently don't work out and have to be changed. They know that planning is difficult, and that the feedback from planning may be delayed for months or years. Successful people are willing to analyze their time and find out how to use it better, even though such an analysis can be difficult and time-consuming.

Successful people do these things—things that they don't like to do—because they know that by doing them they can accomplish their goals. In other words, they do these things because they like the results they obtain. Failures, by contrast, tend to be satisfied with whatever results they can obtain by doing only the things they like to do.

Since success is not a natural state, to be successful you must be different. You must set your sights higher. An American Indian legend tells about a brave who found an eagle's egg and put it into the nest of a prairie chicken. The eaglet hatched with a bunch of chicks and grew up with them. All his life this changeling eagle—thinking he was a prairie chicken—did what the prairie chickens did. He scratched in the dirt for seeds and insects to eat. He clucked and cackled. He flew in a brief flurry of wings and feathers no more than a few feet off the ground. After all, that's how a prairie chicken was supposed to fly.

Years passed. The changeling eagle grew old. One day he saw a magnificent bird far above him in the cloudless sky. Hanging with graceful majesty on powerful wind currents, the bird soared with scarcely a beat of its strong golden wings.

"What a beautiful bird!" said the changeling eagle to his neighbor. "What is it?"

"That's an eagle, the chief of the birds," the neighbor clucked. "But don't give it a second thought. You could never be like him."

So the changeling eagle never gave it another thought. And he died thinking he was a prairie chicken.

It is all too easy to go through life thinking you're a prairie chicken when you might really be an eagle. By doing so, you shortchange yourself and everyone else. Be what you are. Be all you can be. Don't stay on the ground when you can soar. Don't settle for failure when you can have success. How you view yourself plays a vital role in how you choose to spend your time—and your life. Don't sell yourself short when you don't have to.

All of us go into a slump from time to time when the things we do not like to do seem to become more important than our reasons for doing them. Often we find it easier to adjust to the hardships of poor results than to adjust to the hardships of improving results. Just think of all the things that we're willing to do without in order to avoid doing the things we don't like to do!

TIME HABITS AND SUCCESS

Habits are important to success. People form habits, but habits form futures. If you don't form your habits consciously, you will form them unconsciously. And you can only change by changing your habits.

Time use is a habit. To improve, you must discover your present habits and change the ones that need changing. You must clarify your goals. You must continue to ask yourself: "What is the intended result of my action?" You must learn to plan your time every day, every week, every year. You must resolve to use your time better.

Keep in mind, though, that any resolution you make is not worth much unless you keep it. You must stick to your resolution each day and each week until it becomes a habit—until one day you become a different person in a different world, until you have become the master of your likes and dislikes, until you have formed the habit of success.

Your purposes should be practical but also visionary. They should be down to earth but they should also help you achieve your dreams. They should respond to your rational needs as well as to your emotional desires. Your emotional desires keep growing and growing and will push you long after logical needs are met. Logic provides only satisfaction; emotion provides fulfillment.

Start where you are. Evaluate your potential. Then expose yourself to the risks and rewards of achievement. If you don't make a start, you can't possibly get anywhere. Underachievers are not born, they are made. Psychologists have spent years evaluating people's achievement in relation to their potential. They have observed that a lot of people never come close to realizing their potential. Out of this has come the notion that there is hope for underachievers.

If you have been an underachiever, realize that it is possible to reverse the tide of affairs. Find a goal, a purpose in which you have a sincere interest and to which you can devote yourself wholeheartedly. You will be amazed at what you can achieve. Without a goal—and a sincere commitment to it—you will continue to modify your expectations, shifting them to even lower levels of anticipated achievement.

You can change. You can be better. There are several practical things you can do to make a start. Begin right where you are, wherever you choose. Start with simple things. For example:

1. Do something you don't want to do.
2. Do something you do want to do.
3. Spend a few minutes every day in meditation or quiet thought.
4. Be of benefit to someone else every day.
5. Make a list of the things you like to do, the things you want to do, and the things you have done successfully in the past. Compare it with a list of things you don't want to do and things you have not done successfully in the past.

6. Pursue a goal that seems possible for you at this point in your life: You can afford it; you have the time; your family is behind you; it will not conflict with your current responsibilities.
7. Turn off the TV and read a good book instead.
8. Break a habit, any habit.
9. Do something constructive to make yourself a better person. Make the first phone call. Write the first letter. Do whatever it takes to get started. Take one concrete step toward achieving whatever goal you choose.

Ultimately, to be successful—in managing your time or in anything else—you must act. Success demands two things: You must know what to do, and you must do it. There is a big difference between knowing what to do and doing it. Most of us seem to know what to do, but few of us actually do it. As Will Rogers used to say, "It may be common sense, but that doesn't mean it's common practice."

—Finally, if you want to be successful, consistently practice these ten steps for effective time management:

1. Analyze your time. Discover what you do, when you do it, how long you spend doing it, and why you do it.
2. Clarify your objectives and put them in writing. Set your priorities. Make sure you're getting what you really want out of life.
3. Set one major objective every day and form the habit of achieving it.
4. Plan your time every day and every week.
5. Start each day productively. The first hour of your day has a tremendous impact on how the rest of the day goes.
6. Develop the habit of finishing what you have started. Do not jump from one thing to another.
7. Eliminate one time waster from your life every week.
8. Conquer your tendency to procrastinate. Learn to do it now.
9. Reward yourself for achievement. Develop a good self-image.

10. Take time for yourself—time to dream, time to relax, time to live.

Your success in managing your time depends on your ability to define your objectives and your willingness to commit yourself to those objectives. Examine your purposes in life, and make them as large as you can. Big purposes make big people. Remember that you can never succeed beyond the purpose to which you are willing to surrender. And that surrender is never complete until you have formed the habit of doing things that failures don't like to do.

INDEX

accessibility, controlling, 79–80
action vs. thought, 23, 42, 64
activities, administrative
  analyzing importance of, 42–45
  contribution to objectives of, 56
  discrepancies between objectives
    and, 56, 58
  habitual nature of, 47
  nonproductive, *see* time wasters
  physical vs. mental, 23, 42
  pleasant vs. unpleasant, 41
  as priority decisions, 46
  scheduled vs. actual, 75
  sequence of, 41, 68
  site of, 68
  systematic analysis of, 77
  "task jumping" in, 90
  unpleasant, 41, 92–93
  urgent vs. important, 42–44
activity traps, 29–30, 103
  avoiding, 114
  conflicts resulting from, 99
  in-house studies as, 87

management by objectives and,
  29–31
  in personal time, 119–121
adaptability, 6
agendas
  for meetings, 87
  for telephone calls, 81
Aldrin, Buzz, 27
assertiveness training, 91
assumptions
  changing, 18–19
  as deterrents to time manage-
    ment, 17–24
  testing, 18
  unnecessary, 95
authority
  chart of, 109
  clarification of, 85
  degrees of, 108
  delegated, 108

behavior
  analyzing, 15
  habitual, 47

behavior *(continued)*
  impulsive, 75
  modifying, 16
  reinforcement of, 16–17
  see also habit (s)

clutter
  cause of, 94
  reducing, 94–95
commitment, 125–126
committees as time wasters, 86
communications climate, 103
commuting, *see* travel
computerized information systems,
    90
concentration, creating proper
    climate for, 80
conflicts
  activity traps as cause of, 99
  between superior and subordi-
    nate, 99–100
  perceptual, 99–100
  in priorities, 38–40, 98–99
consistency, 16–17
conversations, controlling, 80–81
correspondence, 89
  see also paperwork
cost-effectiveness, 21
crises
  anticipation of, 84
  avoiding, 84
  as impetus for improvement, 84
  patterns of, 22, 84
  planning for, 69
  priority of, 44
  recurring nature of, 84
  time wasters as cause of, 83–84
  unavoidable, 84
  see also urgency
criticism, soliciting, 103, 114

daily planning, 22, 72–74
  mistakes common in, 72, 74
  objectives in, 74
  priorities in, 74

scheduling in, 74–75
  techniques for, 73–74
  time estimates in, 74
daily planning sheet, 73
deadlines
  commitment to, 93
  as incentive, 40, 93
  for objectives, 33
  restructuring, 31
  self-imposed, 93
decision making
  independent, 86
  meetings and, 86
  risk in, 92
delegation
  barriers to successful, 82–83
  definition of, 107
  follow-up in, 110
  guidelines for, 107, 109–110
  improving, 68, 109
  vs. job assignment, 107
  levels of, 108
  as motivation for subordinates,
    83
  of nonessential activities, 97
  organizational climate and, 111
  patterns of, 108–109
  planning in, 110
  psychological factors in, 82–83
  responsibility and, 107
  self-evaluation of, 106–107, 109
  in staff development, 83, 104,
    108
  of telephone responsibilities, 82
  upward, 111
deliberation vs. immediate action,
    22–23
desk (s)
  clutter and, 94
  as work tool, 95
detail, excessive
  causes of involvement in, 82
  time log in reflecting, 83
  as time waster, 44

dialogue
  in conflict prevention, 99, 100
  in determining priorities, 40
  in time management, 103
dictation, 89
  while traveling, 96
dictation equipment, 89, 96
discarding, importance of, 95
distractions, *see* interruptions
Douglass's Law, 94
Drucker, Peter, 13, 21

efficiency vs. effectiveness, 21
80–20 rule, 45, 121
emergencies, *see* crises
example, administrator as, 102,
    109, 113
expectations, clarifying, 99

fears, vague
  overcoming, 94
  procrastination resulting from,
    93–94
filing system (s) , 95
flexibility, 75
follow-up
  in delegation, 110
  to meetings, 87

goals, personal
  daily involvement in, 123
  family role in, 122
  planning for, 122
  priorities among, 121
  realistic, 120
  setting, 119–120
  subgoals as approach to, 122–123
  time and, 117
  time schedule for, 120
  visionary nature of, 131
government control
  in hospital administration, 11–12
  planning necessitated by, 64
group time management, 100–104,
    113–114

cooperation in, 104
productivity resulting from,
    103–104
requisites for, 102
staff development and, 102
staff dialogue concerning, 100–
    101
time waster profiles in, 100–101,
    113
workshops in, 104
see also time management
group time waster profile, 100–101

habit (s)
  awareness of, 47–62
  beneficial effects of, 14–15
  changing, 15–17, 97
  defined, 13
  formation of, 15–17, 130
  harmful effects of, 13–15
  identifying, 15–16
  as learned behavior, 15
  procrastination as, 94
  reinforcement of, 16–17, 97
  success as, 131
  in time allocation, 47
  time wasters as, 13–14, 97
  see also behavior
hard work, myth of, 20–21
health care
  administrators as role models in,
    3
  cost of, 11–12
hospital administration
  complexity of, 11
  management challenge of, 7
hospital administrators
  demands on, 3–4, 11–12
  dependence of, on staff, 98
  duties of, 12
  as examples to staff, 102, 109,
    113
  physical fitness and, 3
  as role models in health care, 3

hospitals
  government control and, 11–12,
    64
  legislation and, 11–12
human interactions, priority of, 20

improvement
  commitment to, 104, 126
  praising, 114
  setting objectives for, 114
impulsive behavior, controlling,
    75
indecision, 92
  see also decision making
information
  collecting, 89, 92
  increase of, 88
insecurity
  delegation and, 82–83
  socializing and, 81
interruptions
  analyzing, 51
  controlling, 79–81
  minimizing, 68, 81
  as routine, 44
  staff as cause of, 80
  time log of, 60

James, William, 14
job assignment vs. delegation, 107
job descriptions, 85
job function (s)
  analysis of, see job function
    analysis
  perceptions of, 48
job function analysis
  description of, 48–49
  purpose of, 56
  sample of, 55
  time log as approach to, 50–51
  worksheet for, 49

Landers, Ann, 123–124
Lao-tzu, 98
limitations, recognition of, 91

McKay, James, 12
mail, screening of, 95
mailing lists, 88, 94
"Making Habits Work for You"
    (James), 15
Management and the Activity
    Trap (Odiorne), 30, 99
management by objectives (MBO)
  activity traps and, 29–31
  weakness of, 29
Management of Time, The
    (McKay), 12
MBO (management by objec-
    tives), see management by
    objectives
meetings
  agendas for, 87, 88
  analysis of, 87
  attendance at, 87
  as avoidance of issues, 86–87
  follow-up to, 87, 88
  minutes of, 87
  as routine, 44
  time limits for, 87
  time log of, 61
  as time wasters, 86–88
  unnecessary, 86
memos, 88–89
mistakes, 92
mornings, significance of, 14, 22,
    75, 90
motivation, 83
Murphy's Laws, 63, 69–70

objectives
  change in, 26
  clarification of, 17, 32, 34–35
  commitment to, 32
  compatibility among, 32, 34
  daily consideration of, 28–29, 31
  deadlines for, 33
  defining, 26–27
  discrepancies between activities
    and, 56, 58
  lack of, 85–86

long-range, 28–31
losing sight of, 30
motivation and, 32
planning and, 65
projection of, 28–29
pyramid model for, 28–29
qualification of, 33
realistic, 32–33
self-determined, 31–32
specific nature of, 27, 33
stability, personal, and, 27
staff involvement in, 32
time loss from lack of, 85
time schedules for, 33, 34–35
writing of, 30, 31–32, 34
see also goals, personal; management by objectives (MBO)
obstacles
anticipating, 128
fear of, 93–94
Odiorne, George, 30, 99
office, arrangement of, 80–81
open-door policy, 79–80
opportunities, taking advantage of, 23–24, 65
organizational climate, delegation and, 111
overextension, 90–91
overwork
causes of, 19, 21, 44
dangers of, 123–124
solutions to, 19
as threat to personal time, 117

paperwork, 4, 89, 94–95
reducing, 88–90
as time waster, 44
see also mail; reading
Pareto, Vilfredo, 45
Pareto's Principle, 45–46, 121
Parkinson's Law, 36
patterns
in crises, 22, 84
in daily activities, 22

in delegation, 108–109
in time loss, 14
perfectionism, 89, 93
performance evaluation
priorities and, 39–40
time habits and, 114
persistence, 126, 130–131
personal time, 115–124
activity traps in, 119, 121
amount of, 117
analysis of, 117–119
balancing work time and, 56, 123–124
goals and, 117
habit in, 118
loss of, to work time, 56
planning of, 116–117
random patterns of, 116
self-knowledge and, 116
similarities between work time and, 116
physical fitness, 3
planning
vs. chance, 86
daily, *see* daily planning
definition of, 65
experimentation with, 85
forms for, 67, 73
as a habit, 66
importance of, 63–64, 85
lack of, 71–72
objectives and, 65
options in, 71
of personal time, 116–117
priorities in, 68–72
as a priority, 44
purpose of, 72
resistance to, 21–22, 44, 63–65
scheduling in, 65
success despite lack of, 64, 86
systematic approach to, 66–68
time as element in, 65, 69–71
time log (s) in, 69–71
uncontrollable events and, 69
universal applicability of, 85

planning (*continued*)
  value of, 72
  weekly, 66–72
  see also objectives; priorities
planning sheets
  daily, 73
  weekly, 67
potential, personal
  evaluating, 131
  realizing, 129–133
praise, importance of, 114
pressure
  job performance and, 40
  procrastination as cause of, 92–
    93
  reactions to, 20
priority (ies)
  acting on, 90, 96
  conflicts in, 98–99
  conscious determination of, 37
  criteria used in determining, 38
  decisions about, 4
  definition of, 37
  dialogue concerning, 40, 114
  establishing, 17, 68, 85–86
  evaluation of, 39–46
  identifying, 95
  importance of, 68
  lack of, 85–86
  planning as, 44
  staff development as, 102
  superiors, effect of, on, 39, 91
  unconscious determination of,
    37, 42
  urgency as factor in determin-
    ing, 42
proaction vs. reaction, 65
problems
  anticipating, 72
  identifying, 22
  obstacles to solving, 22
problems, solving
  instructing staff in, 11
  obstacles to, 22

procrastination
  coping with, 30–31, 93, 94
  crises resulting from, 83–84
  fear as cause of, 91–92
  reasons for, 92–94
  socializing as factor in, 81
  in staff development, 113
productivity
  group time management and,
    103
  time management workshops
    and, 104
progress, 7
  monitoring, 126–128
  recording, 127
punctuality, 87, 88

quiet hour, 80, 94

reaction
  as managerial style, 64–65
  vs. proaction, 65
reading
  lack of time for, 4
  selectivity in, 89
  techniques for, 89
  as time waster, 45
  while traveling, 96
report cycles, 89
reports
  evaluating necessity of, 89
  oral vs. written, 89
  procrastination in writing, 93
  recording equipment for, 89
  see also paperwork
response patterns, *see* habits
responsibilities
  chart of, 109
  clarification of, 85
  conflicting views of, 99
  delegation and, 107
  hierarchy of, 107–108
responsibility–authority chart, 109
rewards as incentive
Rogers, Will, 132

routine tasks
  analysis of, 97
  eliminating, 96–97
  minimizing, 45
  as time wasters, 97
  urgency of, 44

scheduling
  guidelines for, 74–75
  objectives and, 74
  in planning, 65
  in time management, 17
  written, 74
secretaries
  duties of, 75
  importance of, 112
  instruction of, 113
  at meetings, 87, 112
  relationship with administrators, 112
  role of, 112–113
  telephone responsibilities of, 81
self-discipline, 3, 85
self-evaluation
  of delegation, 106–107, 109
  of time management, 7–10
  of time wasters, 100–101
self-knowledge, 116
self-reward as incentive, 93
seminars in time management, 104
  see also time management workshops
socializing
  insecurity as factor in, 81
  as time waster, 13–14, 81
spontaneity, 23–24, 65
staff
  avoiding time loss among, 100–101
  development of, see staff development
  dialogue with, 100–103
  interruptions caused by, 80–81
  motivation of, 83
  temporary, 71

time waster profiles for, 100–101
workshops on time management for, 104
see also secretaries
staff development
  guidelines for, 113–114
  as priority, 44, 102, 113
  requirements for, 102
  time management in, 102, 113
stress, 21, 117
studies, in-house, 81
subscriptions, 89
success
  activities contributing to, 129
  as a habit, 131
  reasons for, 128–129
  time management as factor in, 125, 131
summaries, value of
  at meetings, 87
  in reports, 89

"task jumping," 90
telephone calls
  agenda for, 81
  consolidating, 81
  delegation of responsibility for, 81, 82
  ending, 82
  planning, 81
  scheduling, 81–82
  screening, 81
  time limits for, 82
  time log of, 59
  as time wasters, 44, 81–82
telephone company, 82
temporary staff, 71
tension, 21, 93, 117
  thinking as crucial activity, 4, 23, 42, 64, 75, 95
time
  allocation of, see time allocation
  analyzing use of, 17, 47–62
  assumptions about, 17–19
  available, 41

time *(continued)*
  characteristics of, 5–6, 12–13
  controllable, 69
  defined, 12–13
  estimating allotment of, 34–35,
    68–71, 91
  management of, *see* time man-
    agement
  minimum requirements of, 69,
    91
  obsession with, 115
  paradox of, 5, 115
  personal, *see* personal time
  planning use of, *see* planning;
    time plans
  reallocation of, 19–20
  required vs. available, 69–71
  as a resource, 5
  uncontrollable, 69, 126
time allocation
  analysis of, 48–62
  criteria for, 38
  habit in, 47, 130
  importance of, 4–5
  personal discretion in, 58
  see also planning; priorities
time log (s)
  analysis of, 56–58
  daily, 50–54
  detail, preoccupation with,
    reflected in, 83
  duration of, 57
  impartial observer as keeper of,
    57–58
  for interruptions, 58, 60
  in job function analysis, 50–51
  for meetings, 58, 61
  method for keeping, 50–51
  periodic use of, 57, 58
  in planning, 22, 50
  sample, 52–53, 59–61
  specialized, 58–61
  summarizing, 51, 54
  for telephone calls, 58–59
  for visitors, 58, 60

time loss
  objectives, lack of, and, 85
  patterns in, 14
  see also time wasters
time management
  action plan for, 128
  assumptions about, 18–25
  benefits of, 127–128
  commitment to, 126
  delegation and, 83
  essentials of, 132–133
  motivation for, 6, 24–25, 125
  objectives and, 27–28, 56
  obstacles, anticipation of, in, 128
  persistence in, 126
  personal time and, 115
  progress in, 126–128
  secretaries and, 113
  self-evaluation of, 7–10
  as self-management, 6, 13
  staff dialogue concerning, 114
  success as result of, 125
  systematic approach to, 17
  workshops in, *see* time manage-
    ment workshops
  see also group time management
time management workshops
  for administrators, 103–104
  benefits of, 103–104
  evaluating potential usefulness
    of, 105
  for staff, 104
time plan (s)
  daily, 73
  samples of, 70, 73
  weekly, 70
time use
  analysis of, 17, 47–62
  awareness, lack of, in, 47
  evaluating, 17
  staff discussion of, 101
time wasters
  analyzing, 76–79
  common, 79, 100–101
  eliminating, 97

externally imposed, 77
as habits, 97
identifying, 45, 58, 76–79
in-house studies as, 87
meetings as, 86–88
paperwork as, 88–90
prevalence of, 77
profile of, 101
reports as, 89
routine tasks as, 97
self-imposed, 77–78
social interactions as, 13–14
staff dialogue concerning, 100–101
systematic approach to, 77–79
telephone calls as, 81
time log in revealing, 58, 78
travel
as productive time, 75, 96
as routine, 44
trips, *see* travel
trivia, eliminating, 96
trust in delegation, 108, 111

underachievers, 131
urgency
analysis of, 42–43
demands resulting from, 42
vs. importance, 42–45
priorities, effect on, of, 42–43
of routine tasks, 44–45
time allocation and, 42–45

visitors, drop-in
controlling, 80–81
time log of, 60
as time wasters, 79

weekly planning, 66–72
word processing systems, 35–36, 90
work flow, analysis of, 21, 113
workshops, *see* time management
workshops
worry list, 94
writing, effective, 89

Xerox Corporation, 88